Be My Disciples

Peter M. Esposito
President

Jo Rotunno, MA
Publisher

Anne P. Battes, M.Ed.
Associate Publisher

Program Advisors
Michael P. Horan, PhD
Elizabeth Nagel, SSD

GRADE TWO
SCHOOL EDITION

"The Subcommittee on the Catechism, United States Conference of Catholic Bishops, has found this catechetical series, copyright 2014, to be in conformity with the *Catechism of the Catholic Church*."

NIHIL OBSTAT
Rev. Msgr. Robert Coerver
Censor Librorum

IMPRIMATUR
† Most Reverend Kevin J. Farrell DD
Bishop of Dallas
March 5, 2013

† In Memoriam

Dedicated to James Bitney, 1947–2013, creative, contributing writer and editor for Grades 1 and 2 of the *Be My Disciples* series as well as many other RCL Benziger curriculum series over the years.

The *Nihil Obstat and Imprimatur* are official declarations that the material reviewed is free of doctrinal or moral error. No implication is contained therein that those granting the *Nihil Obstat and Imprimatur* agree with the contents, opinions, or statements expressed.

Acknowledgments

Toll Free   877-275-4725
Fax   800-688-8356

Visit us at RCLBenziger.com
and BeMyDisciples.com

20762 ISBN 978-0-7829-1635-5 (Student Edition)
20772 ISBN 978-0-7829-1641-6 (Teacher Edition)

1st printing
Manufactured for RCL Benziger in Cincinnati, OH, USA. April, 2013.

Contents

Welcome to
Be My
Disciples!

A Few Facts About Me

My name is _____

My favorite story is _____

My favorite holiday is _____

I am good at _____

New Things to Learn

This year we will learn many new things about God. We will learn more about Jesus and how to celebrate with our Church family.

Play this game with a partner to begin to learn new things. As you come to each section, write the answer to the question.

Unit 1: We Believe, Part One

God is the Father and Creator. He made everyone and everything out of love, without any help.
Write the word that means only God has the power to do everything good. _____

Clue: Look on page 52.

Unit 2: We Believe, Part Two

Jesus is God's own Son. He is the Savior of the world.

Write the word that means "God saves." _____

Clue: Look on page 81.

Unit 3: We Worship, Part One

The Sacraments are seven signs of God's love for us. We share in God's love when we celebrate the Sacraments. Write the word that means to honor and love God above

all else. _____

Clue: Look on page 124.

Unit 4: We Worship, Part Two

At Mass, we listen to God's Word and give thanks to him.

What is a word we sing before the Gospel at Mass? _____

Clue: Look on page 189.

Unit 5: We Live, Part One

We live as children of God when we live the Great Commandment. The Great Commandment sums up all of God's Laws.

What is a sign of how Jesus lived the Great Commandment?

_____

Clue: Look on page 246.

Unit 6: We Live, Part Two

The Our Father is the prayer of the whole Church.

Find the word that means "Yes, it is true. We believe!" _____

Clue: Look on page 323.

Enough for Everyone

Leader We gather to praise your Word, O LORD.

All **Thank you for the gift of your Word.**

Leader A reading from the holy Gospel according to John.

All **Glory to you, O Lord.**

One day a large crowd of people was listening to Jesus. That evening Jesus said, "Where can we get enough food for all these people?" His disciple Andrew said, "There is a boy here with five loaves of bread and two fish, but what good will that do?" Jesus said, "Tell the people to sit down." Then he took the bread and fish and gave thanks to God. He passed out the food to all the people who were there. When everyone was full, he asked the disciples to pick up the food that was left over. They collected twelve baskets of bread   BASED ON JOHN 6:1-13

The Gospel of the Lord.

All **Praise to you, Lord Jesus Christ.**

Leader *Come forward in a line and bow before the Bible.*

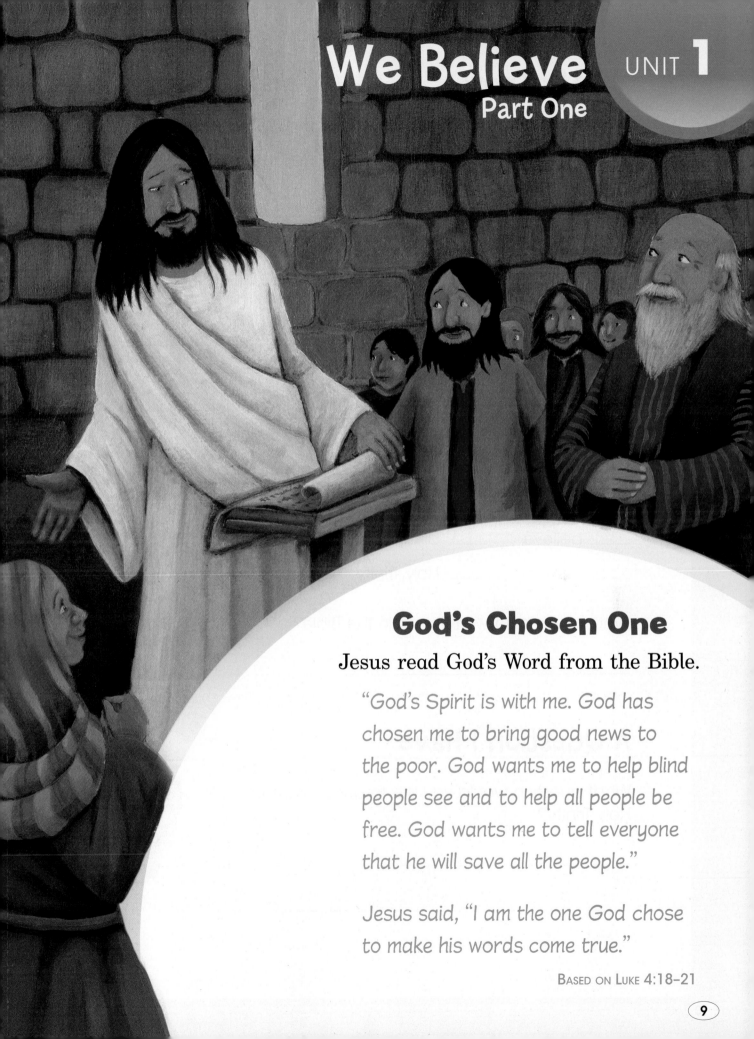

We Believe
Part One

UNIT **1**

God's Chosen One

Jesus read God's Word from the Bible.

"God's Spirit is with me. God has chosen me to bring good news to the poor. God wants me to help blind people see and to help all people be free. God wants me to tell everyone that he will save all the people."

Jesus said, "I am the one God chose to make his words come true."

BASED ON LUKE 4:18–21

(9)

What I Know

What is something you already know about these faith concepts?

The Bible

_____

_____

The Church

_____

_____

*Put an **X** next to the faith words you know. Put a **?** next to the faith words you need to learn more about.*

_____ believe   _____ disciples   _____ Creator

_____ faith   _____ Holy Trinity   _____ soul

Whose words do we listen to in the Bible?

_____

A Question I Have

What question would you like to ask about the Holy Trinity?

_____

_____

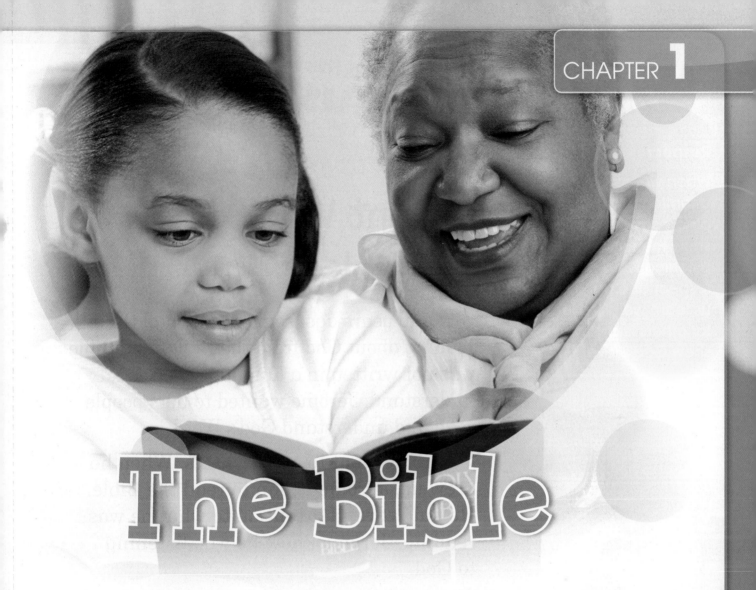

CHAPTER 1

The Bible

? What is your favorite story? What is your favorite Bible story?

When we listen to the Bible we listen to God speaking to us. These are words from the Bible. Listen to what God is telling us.

Long ago, God spoke to people who lived before us. He spoke in many different ways. Now God talks to us through his own Son, Jesus.   BASED ON HEBREWS 1:1–2

? What do you think God is saying to you in these words from the Bible?

Respect

When we pay attention to what others say to us, we show them respect. Listening is a sign of respect and can help us learn well. Respect for others is a way we show God's love.

A Saint Who Loved the Bible

Many years ago, some people had trouble reading about God from the Bible. The Bible was not written in a language they could understand. Jerome wanted to help people read and understand God's Word.

Jerome went to good schools. When he grew up, Jerome began to read the Bible. He paid careful attention to what he was reading. Jerome knew he was listening to God.

Jerome loved the Bible. He loved it so much he wanted other people to love it and read it and learn from it. So Jerome decided to help. Jerome put the Bible in words people could read and understand. Today, we know Jerome as Saint Jerome. We honor him as one of the great teachers of the Church.

❓ How did Jerome help other people read and learn from the Bible?

My Favorite Bible Story

Activity

You can help others understand God's Word in the Bible. Think again about your favorite Bible story. Draw a picture of it here.

Now, find out something important that Saint Jerome said. Learn why it is so important to pay attention to the Bible. Unscramble the letters.

"If you know the _____ ,
              LBBIE

you know _____."
              EJSSU

Faith Words
Bible
The Bible is the written Word of God.

disciples
Disciples are people who follow and learn from someone. Disciples of Jesus follow and learn from him.

A Story About Listening

One day Jesus told this story about listening to the Word of God in the Bible.

"A farmer went to scatter some seeds. Some fell on a path. The birds ate them. Some seeds fell on rocks. They dried up and died. Some seeds fell among thorns. The thorns grew and choked the seeds. Other seeds fell on good soil. They grew strong.

People are like the seeds that the farmer scattered. People who do not listen to God's Word are like the seeds on the path. People who listen to God's Word but soon forget it are like the seeds on the rocks. Some people hear God's Word, but they let worries about other things crowd it out. They are like the seeds among the thorns. Other people hear God's Word and really pay attention. They are like the seeds that fall on good soil. Faith grows in them."

BASED ON MATTHEW 13:3–9, 19–23

The Written Word of God

The **Bible** is a holy book. It is God's own loving Word to us. When we read or listen to the Word of God in the Bible, we listen to God speak to us. In the Bible, God tells us about his great love for us.

God chose special people to write the Bible. God the Holy Spirit helped people write what God wanted to tell us. The Bible has two main parts. The first main part is the Old Testament. The second main part is the New Testament. The New Testament tells about Jesus and his **disciples**.

We are to live as disciples of Jesus. The Bible tells us to follow Jesus. We are to treat others as God wants us to treat them.

? What does God tell us about in the Bible?

Activity

1. Review the Bible story. Put the letter in the box that tells where the seeds fell.

A seeds on rocks   **B** seeds on good soil   **C** seeds on a path

___ They do not listen to God's Word

___ They hear God's Word, but soon forget it.

___ They hear God's Word and listen to it.

2. Share with a partner how people who listen to the Word of God are like the good soil.

Songs in the Bible

The Bible is like a library. It has many books in it. All of the books tell us of God's love for us. One of those books is called the Book of **Psalms.**

The Book of Psalms is in the Old Testament. The writers of the psalms wrote the psalms for people to pray when they were happy and when they were sad. They wrote psalms to help people tell God that they love him. Psalms also help people ask God for what they need. Other psalms were written to help people remember what God did for them and to thank him.

? Why did the writers write the Book of Psalms?

There are 150 psalms in the Book of Psalms. Every psalm is a prayer we can sing.

These words from Psalm 119 praise God and sing about God's Word.

The Word of God makes people joyful.
The Word of God helps people know God.
The Word of God is true and lasts forever.

BASED ON PSALM 119:14, 130, 160

? Why do we pray the psalms?

Activity

Sing a Psalm

Sing the first verse of this psalm to the tune of "Mary Had a Little Lamb." Then use your own words to finish the second verse.

Pay attention to God's Word.
It brings joy,
Hope, and light,
Helping all of us to know
What is true and right.

BASED ON PSALM 119

Pay attention to God's Word.
Then you'll know
What is true.

_____

_____

_____

Faith-Filled People

King David

We read the story of King David in the Old Testament. King David was a musician. He wrote many prayers that were songs. These prayers are called psalms.

The Bible Tells Good News

The **Gospels** are the most important books in the Bible. The Bible has four Gospels. They are in the New Testament.

The Gospels were written by Saint Matthew, Saint Mark, Saint Luke, and Saint John. All four Gospels spread the Good News. The Good News is that God loves us very much.

Each Gospel tells what Jesus said and did. Each Gospel tells how Jesus helped people learn about God. Each Gospel tells what we must do to become Jesus' disciples.

The most important part of the Gospels is the story of Jesus' dying on the Cross and his rising from the dead.

? What is one Gospel story you know about Jesus? What does it tell you about him?

Matthew

Mark

Luke

John

Disciples of Jesus respect others. You are a disciple of Jesus. You can pay attention to God's Word. You can tell others about Jesus. You can help people come to know more about God's great love for them.

I Follow Jesus

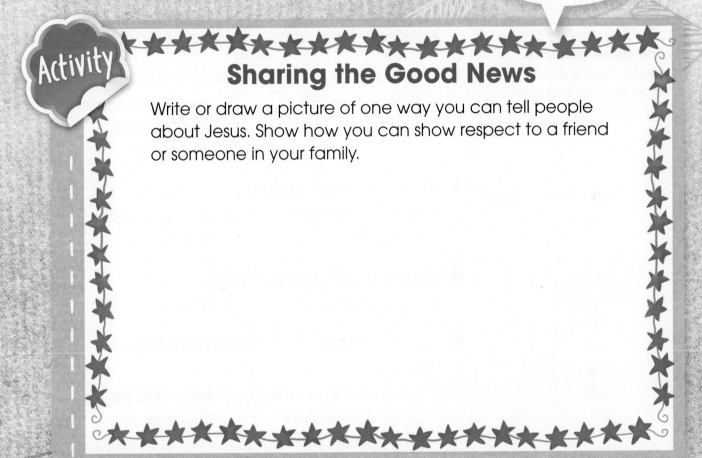

Sharing the Good News

Write or draw a picture of one way you can tell people about Jesus. Show how you can show respect to a friend or someone in your family.

My Faith Choice

This week, I will read from the Bible. I will share with others what I read. I will

_____

_____ .

Pray, "Thank you, Holy Spirit, for helping me to pay attention and learn from the Bible. Amen."

1. The Bible is the written Word of God.

2. In the Bible, God tells us of his love for us.

3. The Bible helps us learn about Jesus and how to live as his disciples.

Chapter Review

Recall

Read each sentence. Draw a line through each ending that does not belong.

1. The Bible is the written
   - history of the world.
   - Word of God.

2. The two main parts of the Bible are the
   - Psalms and the Gospels.
   - The Old Testament and the New Testament.

3. The Gospels tell us about
   - the creation of the world.
   - what Jesus said and did.

4. The Book of Psalms is in the
   - Old Testament.
   - New Testament.

5. The most important part of the Gospels is the story of
   - Jesus' dying on the Cross and his rising from the dead.
   - Jesus and his disciples.

Reflect

How do the Gospels spread the Good News?

_____

_____

Share Share with a friend one way you are a disciple of Jesus.

A Listening Prayer

Pray together. Ask God to help you listen to his Word.

Leader
O God, open our ears to hear you.
Open our hearts to love you.

All
Help us pay attention to your Word.

Leader
Let us lift our voices in song.
Sing the song on page 17.
Now let us listen to God's Word.

Reader
Let the word of Christ dwell in you richly, as in all wisdom you teach . . . one another, singing psalms, hymns, and spiritual songs with gratitude in your hearts to God. And whatever you do, in word or in deed, do everything in the name of the Lord Jesus.

COLOSSIANS 3:16–17

The word of the Lord.

All
Thanks be to God.

Leader
Let us think about what we heard
God saying to us in this reading.
(Pause).
We thank you, O God,
for your Word to us in the Bible,
for the Good News of the Gospels,
and for making us disciples of
Jesus, your Son.

All
**O God, we are happy to hear
your Word and keep it. Amen.**

With My Family

This Week . . .

In Chapter 1, "The Bible," your child learned:

▶ The Bible is the written Word of God. The Old Testament and the New Testament are the two main parts of the Bible.

▶ The Holy Spirit inspired the human writers of the Bible. This means that they wrote what God wished to communicate.

▶ The four accounts of the Gospel are the most important books in the Bible.

▶ Paying attention shows respect.

For more about related teachings of the Church, *see Catechism of the Catholic Church,* 101–114, and the *United States Catechism for Adults* pages 11–32.

■ Sharing God's Word

Choose a favorite story or passage from the Gospels. Invite your child to really listen and pay attention as you read the story to him or her. Afterward, invite your child to tell what she or he heard.

■ Living as Disciples

The Christian home and family is a school of discipleship. Choose one or more of the following activities to do as a family, or design a similar activity of your own.

▶ Display your family Bible in a place of prominence in your home. Gather around the Bible to read the Bible and for family prayer. Read one brief passage each night. Your church bulletin may have the passages that are used at Mass for that day.

▶ Teach your child the good habit of paying attention. Paying attention is a sign of respect. Paying attention enables us to hear God speaking to us. Paying attention makes us aware of people in need and opens us up to reach out to them. That awareness leads us to respond—to act with charity and justice.

■ Our Spiritual Journey

Daily prayer is a vital element in the life of the Catholic family. It is one of the foundational spiritual disciplines of a disciple of Christ. In this chapter, your child prayed and listened to Scripture. This type of prayer is called *lectio divina.* Learn the rhythm of lectio divina and pray this form of prayer often as a family. Read and pray together the prayer on page 21. Then pray the following response from Luke 11:28: *"Blessed are those who hear the word of God and observe it."*

For more ideas on ways your family can live as disciples of Jesus, visit **BeMyDisciples.com**

CHAPTER 2

We Know and Love God

? Who helps you read a story, play a game, or pray?

Listen to these words from the Bible. They ask God to help us come to know him better.

Make known to me your ways, LORD;

teach me your paths. PSALM 25:4

? Who else has helped you come to know and love God?

Hospitality

Jesus tells us to treat all people with hospitality. Hospitality helps us welcome others as God's children. It helps us treat others with dignity and respect.

The Church Follows **Jesus**

Welcome!

It is a great Sunday. The sun is shining. Mr. and Mrs. Chen are standing at the door of Holy Trinity Catholic Church. They are smiling as they greet everyone, one by one, "Welcome! Glad to see you!"

Mr. and Mrs. Chen are ushers who greet the people as they arrive for Mass each Sunday. The Chen family is proud to be a member of Holy Trinity parish.

The Chen family do more than join with other members of Holy Trinity for Mass on Sunday. The Chen children attend Holy Trinity Catholic School. Mrs. Chen is a second grade teacher. Mr. Chen runs the Holy Trinity Community Care Center.

They share food and clothing, books and toys, and other things with families who do not have enough money. Best of all, they treat everyone with respect. They are proud to live as joyful disciples of Jesus.

? In what ways are the Chens good disciples of Jesus?

The Chens are good disciples of Jesus. They show hospitality and invite others to know God better. They treat everyone with respect. They welcome others as God's children.

? In what ways are you a good disciple?

Activity

Color each space that has an X to discover what hospitality means.

Show Respect

Like the Chens, you can help others to know and love God. Tell how you can show hospitality and respect.

To your family

_____

_____

To your friends

_____

_____

Faith Words
believe
To believe in God means to know God and to give ourselves to him with all our heart.

Creation Tells Us About God

The Chens helped people learn about God. God's creation also helps us to come to know and **believe** in him. Creation is everything that God has made. All creation helps us come to know and give glory to God. The Bible tells us:

Let the heavens and the earth sing praise,
the seas and whatever moves in them!

Psalm 69:35

The moon, the stars, and the sun help us come to know God. The snow-covered mountains and the deep blue oceans tell us something about God.

The birds, the fish, and the animals help us come to know God. Fields of crops and beautiful flowers are gifts that remind us of God's goodness. All the good things in the world help us come to know God.

❓ What and who help us to know and believe in God?

People are the most important part of God's creation. All people are created in the image of God. People are signs of God's love.

Our families and people in our Church help us to know God, to love him, and to serve him. But God is the one who best invites us to believe in him. God invites us to know him better and to love and serve him. God invites us to give ourselves to him with all our heart.

❓ How are you a sign of God's love?

Activity

Thank You, God

Finish the prayer.

Thank you, God, for

_____.

Thank you, God, for

_____.

Faith Focus
What does Jesus tell us about God?

Faith Words
▶ **faith**
Faith is a gift from God that makes us able to believe in him.

Jesus Helps Us Know God

Jesus told us the most about God. One day a crowd of people came to Jesus. They wanted to know about God. Jesus told them that people were more important to God than everything else he created. They should believe in God with all their hearts.

Jesus said, "Look at the birds. They have all the food they need. Your Father in heaven takes care of them.

Your Father in heaven knows you. You are more important to God than the birds and all the animals. Trust God. Have faith in him."

BASED ON MATTHEW 6:26–34

? What does the Bible story tell you about God?

In this Bible story, Jesus invites us to have **faith** in God's loving care for us. Faith is God's gift to us. It makes us able to know God and to believe in him. It makes us able to know and believe in what God teaches us. When we say yes to God's invitation to believe in him, we show that we have faith.

 How do you show your faith in God?

Faith-Filled People

Saint Philip the Apostle

Jesus invited Philip to be one of his first followers. Jesus said to Philip, "Follow me." Philip then went to his friend Nathanael and told him about Jesus. Nathanael believed too and became a follower of Jesus.

Activity

Trusting God

Look at the pictures. How are the people in these two pictures showing that they trust in God's love? Draw a picture of yourself that shows how you trust in God's love.

The Church Helps Us Know God

Jesus gave us the Church. The Church is a sign of God's love in the world. The Church is the People of God who believe in Jesus Christ.

We belong to the Catholic Church. The Catholic Church goes all the way back to the time of Jesus and the Apostles. The Church helps us to know God and his love for us. The Church helps us grow in faith.

We grow in faith with the people of our Church in many ways. We grow in faith when we pray together. We grow in faith when we are kind to family, friends, and other people. We grow in faith when we care for God's creation.

We grow in faith when we live our faith with our Church family. When we live our faith, we are signs of God's love for others to see.

? What are the ways that you share your faith with others?

You are a sign of God's love. You can help other people to know and believe in God by what you say and what you do.

One way we live as disciples of Jesus is to practice hospitality. You can invite and welcome others to know and believe in God.

I Follow Jesus

Activity

Signs of God's Love

Who can you invite to learn more about God? Write that person's name on the invitation.

You Are Invited to Believe in God

God Invites

_____

friend's name

to know and believe in him.

My Faith Choice

This week, I will show someone that I have faith and know and love God. I will

_____

_____.

 Pray, "Thank you, Holy Spirit, for the gift of faith. Help me share with others how much you love them. Amen."

1. God invites us to know and believe in him.

2. Jesus, the Son of God, tells us the most about God.

3. God gave us the Church to help us grow in faith.

Chapter Review

Recall

Complete the missing letters in the sentences.

1. Faith is to k _____ o _____ God and to

   b _____ l _____ e _____ _____ in him with all our

   h _____ a _____ ts.

2. _____ e _____ u _____ told us the most about God.

3. The C _____ u _____ c _____ helps us grow in faith.

4. Hospitality helps us treat others with

   re _____ p _____ c _____.

Reflect

What are ways you can grow in faith?

_____

_____

_____

_____

_____

| Share | Write a sentence that tells what faith means to you. Share it with a family member. |

We Believe in God!

Vocal prayers are said aloud with others. An act of faith is a vocal prayer. Pray this act of faith as a class.

Leader Let us tell God we believe in him with all our hearts. Let us pray.

All **God, we believe in you with all our hearts.**

Group 1 God our loving Father, all creation reminds us of your love.

All **God, we believe in you with all our hearts.**

Group 2 Jesus, Son of God, you showed us how much God loves us.

All **God, we believe in you with all our hearts.**

Group 3 God the Holy Spirit, you help us to know and believe in God.

All **God, we believe in you with all our hearts.**

Leader God, thank you for your gift of creation and sending your Son to live among us. Jesus helps us to live as your faithful children.

All **Amen.**

With My Family

This Week . . .

In Chapter 2, "We Know and Love God," your child learned:

▶ Faith is God's gift that makes us able to believe in him. God invites us to believe in him.

▶ All creation, especially our families and people in our Church, help us come to know and believe in God.

▶ Jesus revealed to us the most about God. He is the greatest sign of God's love and invites us to have faith in God.

▶ The virtue of hospitality guides us to share our faith in God with others.

For more about related teachings of the Church, see the *Catechism of the Catholic Church* 50–67, 84–95, and 142–175, and the *United States Catholic Catechism for Adults*, pages 50–53.

■ Sharing God's Word

Read together Matthew 6:26–34, where Jesus invites the people to have faith in God. Or read the adaptation of the story on page 28. Talk about how your family blessings strengthen your faith in God.

■ Living as Disciples

The Christian home and family is a school of discipleship. Choose one of the following activities to do as a family, or design a similar activity of your own.

▶ List some people who help your family come to know and believe in God. Write a note of thanks to each person on the list over the next few weeks.

▶ Identify the ways that your family lives the virtue of hospitality. Help your child grow as someone who is open and welcoming. Do this by the example of your own words and actions.

■ Our Spiritual Journey

Prayer is vital to the Christian life. Conversing with God in prayer can help us find and receive direction for living as a Catholic family. Help your child develop the habit of praying regularly. In this chapter, your child learned to pray an act of faith. Read and pray together the prayer on page 33. Then pray, *"God of hospitality, we have faith in you. Welcome us day by day to an even deeper faith."*

For more ideas on ways your family can live as disciples of Jesus, visit **BeMyDisciples.com**

CHAPTER 3

The Holy Trinity

? What is something you learned recently? Who helped you to learn it?

Jesus wanted us to know something very important about God. Listen to find out who Jesus said would help us. Jesus told his disciples:

> "I will ask the Father to send you the Holy Spirit. He will always be with you as your helper and teacher." BASED ON JOHN 14:25–26

? What did Jesus tell us about God?

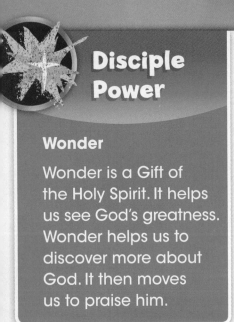

Disciple Power

Wonder

Wonder is a Gift of the Holy Spirit. It helps us see God's greatness. Wonder helps us to discover more about God. It then moves us to praise him.

Many Languages!

People all around the world belong to the Catholic Church. People read the Bible and listen to the words of Jesus in their own languages. They talk with God in prayer in their own languages.

Catholics all over the world pray the prayers of the Mass in their own languages, too. People who speak English begin the Mass, "In the name of the Father, and of the Son, and of the Holy Spirit. Amen."

People who speak Spanish pray, "En el nombre del Padre, y del Hijo, y del Espíritu Santo. Amen."

People who speak Vietnamese pray, "Nhan danh Cha Va Con Va Thanh. Than."

When Catholics all over the world pray the Sign of the Cross, they show that they belong to God's family. They show that they believe what Jesus taught about God.

❓ What does praying the Sign of the Cross show us?

As we say the words of the prayer, we bless ourselves. We touch our forehead, our shoulders, and our chest over our heart. We remember that we are baptized. We show that we belong to God's family.

? When do you pray the Sign of the Cross?

Praying the Sign of the Cross

Draw yourself making the Sign of the Cross. Then learn to pray the Sign of the Cross in a different language. Repeat the words below with your class. Share the prayer with your family.

In the name of the Father,	and of the Son,	and of the Holy Spirit. Amen.
En el nombre del Padre,	y del Hijo,	y del Espíritu Santo. Amen.
Nhan danh Cha	Va Con,	Va Thanh. Than.

Faith Focus
Who is the Third Person
of the Holy Trinity?

Faith Words

Holy Trinity
The Holy Trinity is
One God in Three
Divine Persons—God
the Father, God the
Son, and God the Holy
Spirit.

soul
Our soul is that part of
us that lives forever.

One God

Jesus told us who God is. There is only one God who is God the Father, God the Son, and God the Holy Spirit. We call the One God in Three Persons the **Holy Trinity.** The word *trinity* means "three in one."

God the Father

In the Apostles' Creed, Christians around the world pray, "I believe in God, the Father almighty, Creator of heaven and earth." God the Father is the First Person of the Holy Trinity.

God the Father created everyone and everything out of love. He created all people in his image and likeness. He created each person with a body and a **soul.** The soul is that part of each person that lives forever.

? Who is the Holy Trinity?

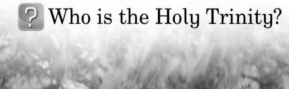

Jesus used the word "Abba" when he prayed to God the Father. The word *Abba* is the word for "father" in the language Jesus spoke. "Abba" means "daddy" in English, "papi" in Spanish, and "ba" in Vietnamese.

Jesus wanted us to know that God the Father loves us and cares for us. He created us to be happy with him now and forever in Heaven.

? What is one way that you can thank God for loving you?

Catholics Believe

Sign of the Cross

We can pray the Sign of the Cross in different ways. Before we listen to the Gospel, we make a small Sign of the Cross on our foreheads, on our lips, and over our hearts.

Activity

Thanking God the Father

We listen to God and thank him. Circle the second letter. Then circle every other letter to find a prayer to God the Father.

L A V B K B W A Q F J A F T L H X E S R

H T L H U A S N L K R Y C O D U G F K

O G R L Y Q O A U T R Z L F O H V K E

_____

_____

Faith Focus
Who is the Second
Person of the
Holy Trinity?

Faith Words
Son of God
Jesus Christ is the Son
of God who became
one of us. He is the
Second Divine Person
of the Holy Trinity.

God the Son

In the Apostles' Creed, we pray that we "believe in Jesus Christ, his only Son, our Lord." The word *Lord* means "God." Jesus is the **Son of God** who became one of us. God the Son is the Second Person of the Holy Trinity.

God the Father loves us very much. He wanted us to know more about him. So he sent his Son to become one of us and to live with us.

In the Apostles' Creed, we also pray that we believe Jesus was "born of the Virgin Mary." We believe that Jesus is both true God and true man. Jesus is the only Son of God the Father. Jesus is also the Son of the Virgin Mary.

❓ What do we pray about Jesus in the Apostles' Creed?

Jesus told us to call God our Father. The Bible tells us we are children of God. We are to live as children of God. Jesus taught us how to do this. He said,

"You shall love the Lord your God,

with all your heart, . . .

You shall love your neighbor as yourself."

MATTHEW 22:37, 39

? How do you show that you love God and others?

Sign Jesus' Message

Sign this message for your family and friends!

Love

God

with

all

your

heart.

Faith Focus
Who is the Third Person
of the Holy Trinity?

God the Holy Spirit

In the Apostles' Creed we pray, "I believe in the Holy Spirit." God the Holy Spirit is the Third Person of the Holy Trinity.

Jesus told us about the Holy Spirit. He said to his disciples,

"The Father in heaven will send you the Holy Spirit."

BASED ON LUKE 11:13

At Baptism the priest or deacon baptizes in the name of the Father, and of the Son, and of the Holy Spirit. This shows that we share in the life of the Holy Trinity.

We first receive the gift of the Holy Spirit at Baptism. The Holy Spirit is always with us. He helps us to know and to love and to serve God better. The Holy Spirit helps us to live as children of God and disciples of Jesus.

? What are three things the Holy Spirit helps us do?

God the Holy Spirit gives you the gift of wonder. The gift of wonder helps you want to know God more. The more you know about God, the more you can tell others about God.

Telling Others About the Holy Trinity

On each leaf of the shamrock, draw or write one thing you can tell others about the Holy Trinity.

Father

Holy Spirit

Son

My Faith Choice

I will tell other people about the Holy Trinity this week. I will

_____

_____.

Pray, "Thank you, Holy Spirit, for the gift of wonder. Thank you for helping me to learn about you. Amen."

1. God is the Holy
Trinity. God the
Father is the First
Person of the
Holy Trinity.

2. God the Son is the
Second Person of
the Holy Trinity.

3. God the Holy Spirit
is the Third Person
of the Holy Trinity.

Chapter Review

Recall

*Complete the sentences. Use the words in the
word box.*

Lord	One	Three	Trinity

1. We believe in the Holy _____.

2. There is _____ God in _____
Divine Persons.

3. The word _____ means God.

Color the 🙂 *if the sentence is true.*

Color the 🙁 *if the sentence is not true.*

4. God creates each person with a body   🙂 🙁
and a soul.

5. God creates us to be happy with him   🙂 🙁
now and in Heaven.

6. Jesus is the Son of God. He is the Third   🙂 🙁
Person of the Holy Trinity.

7. The Holy Spirit helps us know and love   🙂 🙁
God better.

Reflect

How do you show your love for God?

_____

Share	Explain to a classmate how the Holy Spirit helps us.

The Sign of the Cross

*A ritual uses words, gestures, or actions to help us pray.
Pray now using a ritual action.*

Leader   Come forward one at a time. Bow before
the Bible. Trace a cross on your forehead,
your lips, and over your heart.

All   **(Come forward and sign yourself.)**

Leader   Loving God, you are Father.

All   **Thank you for creating us.**

Leader   You are Son.

All   **Thank you for coming among us.**

Leader   You are Holy Spirit.

All   **Thank you for being always with us.**

Leader   Loving God, you are Father, Son,
and Holy Spirit.

All   **Three in one!**

Leader   We praise you, God, and mark
ourselves as your children.

All   **(Pray the Sign of the Cross
in the language you choose.)**

With My Family

This Week . . .

In Chapter 3, "The Holy Trinity," your child learned:

▶ God is the Holy Trinity. The mystery of the Holy Trinity is the mystery of One God in Three Divine Persons: Father, Son, and Holy Spirit.

▶ We could never have come to know this wonderful truth about the identity of God on our own. We only know this about God because he has revealed this about himself in Jesus Christ.

▶ The Church's belief in the mystery of the Holy Trinity is at the heart of the Church's living faith.

▶ Wonder, one of the seven Gifts of the Holy Spirit, urges us to come to know and praise God for who he is.

For more about related teachings of the Church, see the *Catechism of the Catholic Church,* 232–260, and the *United States Catholic Catechism for Adults,* pages 51–53.

■ Sharing God's Word

Read together John 14:26, the promise of Jesus that the Holy Spirit would come to his disciples. Talk about how wonderful it is that Jesus revealed that there is one God who is Father, Son, and Holy Spirit.

■ Living as Disciples

The Christian home and family is a school of discipleship. Choose one of the following activities to do as a family, or design a similar activity of your own.

▶ Awaken your child's awareness of the gift of wonder. Share both your curiosity and your delight in the mystery of God manifested in the world around you. Point out the many elements of God's creation that help you come to know more about him.

▶ Create a Holy Trinity banner. Display it at the entrance to your home. Use it as a reminder that God the Holy Trinity dwells in your home with your family.

■ Our Spiritual Journey

Praying a doxology is an ancient tradition of the Church. A doxology is a prayer giving praise and honor to God. Remind one another that all you say and do is to give glory to God. Pray the Glory Be regularly together with your child.

*Glory be to the Father
and to the Son
and to the Holy Spirit,
as it was in the beginning
is now, and ever shall be
world without end. Amen.*

For more ideas on ways your family can live as disciples of Jesus, visit **BeMyDisciples.com**

CHAPTER 4

God, Our Father

? What are some of the things parents do to show their love for their children?

Listen to what Saint John wrote about God the Father.

> God our Father loves us with a wonderful love! We are so glad to be his children.

BASED ON 1 JOHN 3:1

? What are some ways God the Father shows his wonderful love for you?

Honor

When we honor others, we show respect and value them. We honor God because we are proud to be his children.

A Garden for Others

The students at Saint Augustine's School know how much God loves them. They try their best to live as children of God. They honor God in many ways.

One thing they do together is to grow vegetables and fruit in a garden at their school. They plant the seeds. They harvest the crops. They wash and bag the fruits and vegetables. They take the food to a food bank. This helps to feed people who do not have enough to eat.

As they work in the garden, the children feel close to God. They show their love for God the Creator and people when they take care of creation. They show they are proud to be children of God.

[?] How do you show that you are proud to be a child of God?

Caring for Creation

When the students of St. Augustine's School tend the garden, they are taking care of creation. See the word *CREATION* below. Think of something in creation that begins with each letter. Write the words on the lines. The first one is done for you.

C clouds

R _____

E _____

A _____

T _____

I _____

O _____

N _____

Draw yourself in this photo
caring for creation.

God, the Creator

You are getting to know more and more about God. God is the Father and the **Creator.** He made everyone and everything out of love and without any help. He made the creatures we can see and the angels we cannot see.

God tells us that he alone is the Creator. He tells us this in the first story in the Bible.

In the beginning, God created the heavens and the earth. He made the sun, the other stars, and the moon. He made the sky, the earth, and the sea.

God made plants, trees, and flowers. He made all the fish and the birds. He made all the animals and other creatures that live on the land. Then God created people in his image and likeness. God looked at all that he had created. He saw that it was very good.

BASED ON GENESIS 1:1, 7–12, 16, 20–21, 24–25, 27, 31

? Which part of God's creation was made in his image and likeness?

God's Creation

God made everything. Draw pictures for this rebus to retell the creation story.

God made _____. This is good!
(Earth)

God made _____. This is good!
(stars and moon)

God made _____. This is good!
(animals)

God made _____. This is good!
(people)

God looked at everything he had made, and he found it very good.

GENESIS 1:31

Faith Words
almighty
God alone is almighty. This means that only God has the power to do everything good.

God the Almighty

We can learn a lot about God when we look at creation. We can come to know that God is good. We can see how much God loves us. The Bible tells us:

Our God is good to all. God loves and cares for every creature.

BASED ON PSALM 145:9

We can also learn that God is **almighty.** The Bible says:

O Lord God Almighty, there is no one and nothing like you!

BASED ON PSALM 89:9

This means that only God has the power to do everything. And everything God does is very good.

God tells us that he does everything out of love. He is always good and loving. We believe in and love God the Father with all our hearts.

We show God and others our trust and love for him by what we say and do. When we do and say things that show we love God, we are signs of God's love for others to see.

? **Why did God create us?**

52

Activity

Find Words About God

Find and circle the words in the puzzle that tell about God. What does each word tell you about God?

Creator Father Almighty Love Good

```
C  B  G  O  O  D  R  D  G  O  D
A  Z  D  X  U  H  S  G  B  E  Q
K  X  E  L  M  K  B  D  C  X  W
L  F  J  A  L  M  I  G  H  T  Y
C  R  E  A  T  O  R  V  G  N  K
I  K  Y  Z  L  O  V  E  F  B  R
X  B  F  A  T  H  E  R  Y  Q  F
```

Faith-Filled People

Saint Bonaventure

Bonaventure looked at creation and came to know and love God. He said that creation was like a mirror. Whenever he looked at creation, Bonaventure saw and believed that God was good and loving. The Church celebrates the feast day of Saint Bonaventure on July 15.

God Our Father

Jesus told us the most about God. One day, Jesus' friends asked him to teach them to pray. He taught them to pray:

Our Father in heaven,
   hallowed be your name.

MATTHEW 6:9

The word *hallowed* means "very holy." We give great honor to God when we say, "hallowed be your name."

Jesus taught that God his Father is our Father. God the Father loves and cares for us. He knows what we need before we ask for it. God always does what is best for us. We are to believe in him and trust him. We are to honor God as Jesus did.

? What did Jesus teach us about God the Father?

God created everyone and everything out of love. God shares the gift of his love with you every day. You can give honor to God the Father by caring for creation.

I Follow **Jesus**

 **Activity**

Proud to Be a Child of God

How can your class show that you are proud to be children of God? Write or draw your ideas here.

 **My Faith Choice**

This week, I will honor God by showing my love for creation. I will

_____

_____.

 Pray, "Thank you, God the Holy Spirit, for helping me to honor God the Father by caring for creation. Amen."

1. God is the Creator. He made everyone and everything because of his love.

2. God is almighty. He alone can do everything good.

3. Jesus taught us that God the Father is our Father.

Chapter Review

Recall

Complete the crossword puzzle.

Across

2. Creation is a sign of God the ____.

4. The word *hallowed* means very ____.

Down

1. God the ____ made everyone and everything out of love.

3. Jesus taught us to ____ the Our Father.

Reflect

What does it mean that God does everything out of love?

_____

_____

_____

_____

_____

_____

Share Why does Jesus want us to call God, "Father?" Tell your class.

The Lord's Prayer

Christians pray the Lord's Prayer every day.
Pray the Lord's Prayer together.

All

**Our Father, who art in heaven,
hallowed be thy name;
thy kingdom come,
thy will be done
on earth as it is in heaven.
Give us this day our daily bread,
and forgive us our trespasses,
as we forgive those who trespass
   against us;
and lead us not into temptation,
   but deliver us from evil.
Amen.**

Leader

Now let us offer one another a sign
of peace. This action shows that God
is our Father and we are all children
of God.

All

*(Share a sign of peace with one
another).*

With My Family

This Week . . .

In Chapter 4, "God, Our Father," your child learned:

▶ God is the Creator of all that exists. God alone made everyone and everything out of love without any help.

▶ We call God almighty because he has the power to do everything that is good. His power is universal, loving, and merciful.

▶ God is the origin of all that exists. God loves and cares for us.

▶ We honor God the Father when we join in caring for his creation.

▶ When we honor someone, we show them the love and respect that they deserve.

For more about related teachings of the Church, see the *Catechism of the Catholic Church*, 268–274, 279–314, and 325–349, and the *United States Catholic Catechism for Adults*, pages 50–54.

■ Sharing God's Word

Read together the Bible story in Matthew 6:9–13 where Jesus teaches his friends how to pray. Emphasize that Jesus taught us to pray the Our Father, also called the Lord's Prayer.

■ Living as Disciples

The Christian home and family is a school of discipleship. Choose one or more of the following activities to do as a family, or design a similar activity of your own.

▶ Draw a creation mural. Write "God the Creator" at the top of the mural. Decorate the mural with pictures of God's creation. If you have photos from family trips to a park, a zoo or camping, use them with your child to talk about the beauty of creation and add them to the mural.

▶ By your example, help your child honor God's creation. Demonstrate how you use water, energy, food, and your treatment of living creatures. Model respect for all people. Decide as a family what you can do together.

■ Our Spiritual Journey

In the Sermon on the Mount, Jesus gave his disciples guidelines for living as his disciples. He taught them to pray the Lord's Prayer. In this chapter, your child prayed the Lord's Prayer. Pray the Lord's Prayer together as a family this week at bedtime. If you know the prayer in another language besides English, help your child learn it and pray it with you.

For more ideas on ways your family can live as disciples of Jesus, visit **BeMyDisciples.com**

Pick Up and Clean Up

The whistle blew loudly. It was Mr. Gomez, the school principal. He wanted the children's attention at the end of the lunch period on Field Day. "Look around you," he said. "How many pieces of trash do you see?"

The children looked. There was trash everywhere, even in the bushes.

"We have a problem," Mr. Gomez announced. "First, I want you to pick up all this trash, please. Then I want you to go back to your classroom and come up with a plan. Our school yard can be beautiful, but everyone needs to take care of it."

WE ARE CARETAKERS OF GOD'S CREATION

When we look at God's creation, we learn about God. We have a special duty to care for God's creation. It is one way we can honor and show our love for God.

Making Connections

We can do our part to take care of God's creation. The school yard is a good place to start. Develop a plan.

with Math and Science

Pretend you are in a helicopter looking down at your school. Draw a map of what you see with the buildings and the outside areas. Divide the map into sections. Chart the sections. Assign each grade one section to care for. Make a color key to color each grade's section on your map. Find out if there are trash cans in each section. How many more trash cans are needed?

with Language Arts

Talk about how each grade can keep its area clean. Make a list of three ideas. People need reminders that being caretakers of God's creation is our responsibility. Create slogans for a "Keep Our School Clean" campaign.

with Creative Arts

Design "Caretakers of God's Creation" posters to display in each classroom and on school bulletin boards. Use the slogans and simple tips for keeping the school clean. Take before and after pictures. Then with your teacher's help, upload them to your school's Web site. Show how taking care of God's creation makes a difference at your school.

Faith Action

I am God's creation caretaker. Here is one way that I am going to take care of God's creation in my neighborhood.

_____

_____.

Unit 1 Review

A. Choose the Best Word

Complete the sentences. Color the circle next to the best choice for each sentence.

1. The _____ is One God in Three Divine Persons.

○ Holy Trinity   ○ Holy Spirit   ○ Holy Family

2. God the Father is the _____ who made everyone and everything out of love.

○ Apostle   ○ Creator   ○ Holy Spirit

3. Jesus is the _____ Person of the Holy Trinity.

○ First   ○ Second   ○ Third

4. The part of us that lives forever is called the _____.

○ heart   ○ mind   ○ soul

5. We honor the Holy Trinity when we pray the _____.

○ Hail Mary   ○ Sign of the Cross   ○ Lord's Prayer

B. Show What You Know

There is One God in Three Divine Persons. Match the numbers in Column A with the letters in Column B.

Column A	Column B
___ **1.** God the Father	**a.** Savior
___ **2.** God the Son	**b.** Creator
___ **3.** God the Holy Spirit	**c.** Helper

C. Connect with Scripture

What was your favorite story about Jesus in this unit?
Draw something that happened in the story.
Tell your class about it.

D. Be a Disciple

1. *What Saint or holy person did you enjoy hearing about in this unit? Write the name here. Tell your class what this person did to follow Jesus.*

_____

_____

2. *What can you do to be a good disciple of Jesus?*

_____

_____

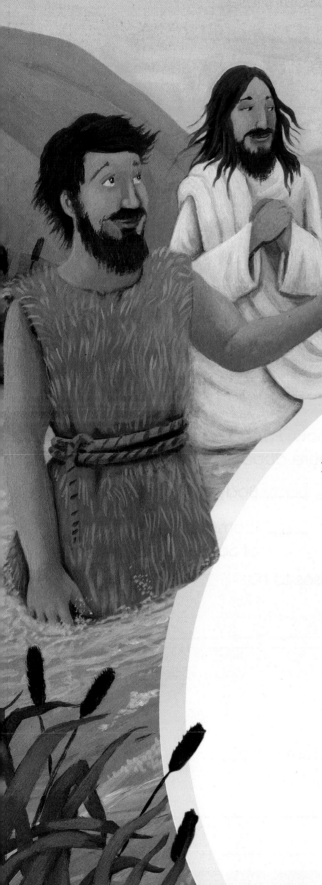

John Baptizes Jesus

John the Baptist was baptizing people in the Jordan River.

"Someone is coming soon," John said. "You must get ready for him. Sin no more."

One day, Jesus himself came to John. John baptized Jesus. Then a voice from heaven said of Jesus, "This is my Son whom I love."

John said to the people, "Look, this is the one God promised to send. He is the Son of God."

BASED ON MATTHEW 3:2–3, 13, 15, 17 AND JOHN 1:29, 34

What I Know

What is something you already know about these faith concepts?

Jesus Christ

_____

_____

The Holy Spirit

_____

_____

The Mother of the Church

_____

_____

*Put an **X** next to the faith words you know. Put a **?** next to the faith words you need to learn more about.*

_____ Resurrection   _____ Pentecost   _____ Body of Christ

_____ Covenant   _____ Ascension   _____ Communion
                                                      of Saints

What do you know about God's promises to his people in the Bible?

_____

A Question I Have

What question would you like to ask about living as a member of the Church?

_____

_____

CHAPTER 5

Jesus, Son of God

? Why is it important to keep a promise?

God made this promise to his people.
He said a child would be born to them.

A virgin will have a baby. They will name him
Wonder-Counselor, God-Hero, Father-Forever,
and Prince of Peace. The child will grow up and
begin rebuilding a world of kindness and love.

BASED ON ISAIAH 7:14; 9:5-6

? Who is the child God promised?

Mercy

Jesus said, "Blessed are people of mercy." Mercy means great kindness. Mercy helps us act with great kindness toward others no matter what.

The Church Follows **Jesus**

Brother Martin

Jesus is the child God promised would be born. Jesus taught us how to build a world of kindness, love, and mercy.

Martin de Porres listened to Jesus. He did what Jesus asked his followers to do. Martin joined a group of religious brothers and promised to show people the kindness and love of God.

Brother Martin lived in the country of Peru in South America. He showed people that God always loves them.

Brother Martin cared for sick people. He brought them food and medicine. He helped find homes for children who had no parents. He brought food and clothes to people who did not have the money to buy them for themselves.

All these things Brother Martin did are called Works of Mercy. When we do show mercy, we share God's love with others.

? What are the Works of Mercy that Martin did to help others?

Acting with Mercy

When we act with mercy, we are working to build a world of kindness and love. We are doing what Jesus taught us to do. We are following in the footsteps of Brother Martin.

Activity

Follow the footprints. Color the footprints that contain acts of mercy. Draw an X through the footprints that do not show acts of mercy.

Visit people who are sick.

Do not share treats with your sister.

Bring clothes to a homeless shelter.

Talk back to your parents.

Help serve dinner to hungry people.

Always want to be first.

Write how the people in the picture are building a world of mercy. Write one more way that you could help.

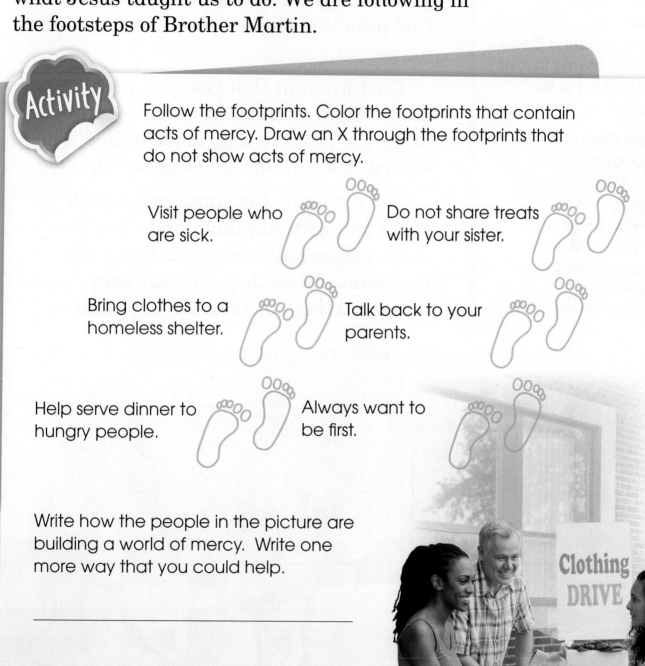

Clothing DRIVE

_____

_____

_____

_____

Faith Words
Covenant
The Covenant is God's promise always to love and be kind to his people.

Jesus Christ
Jesus Christ is the Son of God. He is the Second Person of the Holy Trinity who became one of us. Jesus is true God and true man.

God's Special Promise

The Bible tells us about a very special promise God made with his people. This promise is the **Covenant**. In the Covenant God promised to always love and be kind to his people.

The Covenant that God and people made began at creation. Our first parents broke the promise they made to God. They sinned. We call this sin Original Sin.

God made the Covenant again with Noah and with Abraham and with Moses. God's people still sometimes broke the Covenant. When they did, God sent people to remind them to keep the Covenant.

Still, God's people continued to break the Covenant. God then promised to send someone to make God and people friends again. God kept his promise. He sent his Son, **Jesus Christ**.

Jesus is the Second Person of the Holy Trinity who became one of us. Jesus is true God and true man.

? Why did God send his Son, Jesus?

Catholics Believe

Works of Mercy

The Church teaches us the Works of Mercy. They are ways to be as kind and loving to people as Jesus.

 Activity

Keeping a Promise

Use this code to discover who Jesus is.

The Birth of Jesus

The Bible tells about the birth of Jesus. We call this story the Nativity.

Narrator   Just before Jesus' birth, Joseph and Mary traveled to Bethlehem. Mary and Joseph stopped to find a room in an inn.

Action   *Joseph knocks on the door of the inn. The innkeeper opens the door.*

Joseph   My wife and I need a room. She is going to have a baby.

Innkeeper   There are no rooms left. You may stay in the stable.

Narrator   Mary and Joseph went to the stable. Jesus was born there.

BASED ON LUKE 2:4–7

The Bible tells us that angels told shepherds about the birth of Jesus. The shepherds went to see Baby Jesus. They were filled with joy. They praised God for what they heard and saw.

? What do we call the story of Jesus' birth?

Create a rebus story to show how God kept his promise to send someone to make people friends with God again.

Long ago, [____] and Joseph

came to the little town of Bethlehem. They

had to stay in a stable. There, [____]

was born. Some shepherds were watching

their [____] . Suddenly an

[____] came to them and

told them about the special baby. The

shepherds went and found the baby Jesus

lying in a [____]  .

 angel

 sheep

 Jesus

 manger

 Mary

God Cares for All People

The New Testament tells us that when Jesus grew up, he traveled from place to place. Sometimes he walked. Sometimes he rode a donkey. Sometimes he rode in a boat.

All the things Jesus said and did taught people about God's mercy and love. Mercy means "great kindness." Read this Bible story about God's mercy.

Many people had followed Jesus all day. As nighttime came, Jesus saw that the people were hungry. But there were only two fish and five loaves of bread to feed all the people. This is what Jesus did:

Taking the five loaves and the two fish, and looking up to heaven, he said the blessing, broke the loaves, and gave them to the disciples, who in turn gave them to the crowds. They all ate and were satisfied, and they picked up the fragments left over.

MATTHEW 14:19–20

? In what way did Jesus show that God is kind to people?

Jesus is the greatest sign of God's love and mercy. You can be a follower of Jesus. You can be a sign of God's love and mercy, too.

I Follow Jesus

Activity

Signs of God's Love and Mercy

Look at the pictures. How are the people caring for others? Write in each bubble what the helping person might be saying.

My Faith Choice

This week, I promise to live as a sign of God's love and mercy. I will

_____

_____.

Pray, "Thank you, Holy Spirit, for helping me to live as a sign of God's love and kindness. Amen."

1. The Covenant is a promise of God's love and mercy.

2. The birth of Jesus Christ, the Son of God, is called the Nativity.

3. Everything Jesus said and did shows us God's love and mercy.

Chapter Review

Recall

Match the words to their meanings.

_____ **1.** Mary

_____ **2.** Nativity

_____ **3.** Joseph

_____ **4.** Jesus

a. This Person is the Son of God.

b. She is the Mother of the Son of God.

c. He is the foster father of Jesus.

d. This is the name we give to the Bible story of Jesus' birth.

Add letters to complete the words in the sentences.

6. God's promise to always love and be kind to his people is called the

C ____ ____ ____ ____ ____ ____ t.

7. J ____ s ____ ____ is the Son of God.

8. Jesus showed us God's love and

m ____ ____ ____ y.

Reflect

What are the ways that you show God's love and mercy to others?

_____

_____

Share   Share with your class how you know God loves you.

The Angelus

The Angelus is a prayer that praises God for the birth of Jesus.

Group 1 The angel spoke God's message to Mary,

Group 2 and she conceived of the Holy Spirit.

All **Hail, Mary, full of grace,
the Lord is with thee.
Blessed art thou among women,
and blessed is the fruit of thy
      womb, Jesus.
Holy Mary, Mother of God,
pray for us sinners,
now and at the hour of our death.
Amen.**

Group 1 "I am the lowly servant of the Lord:

Group 2 let it be done to me according to your word."

All **Hail, Mary . . .**

Group 1 And the Word became flesh

Group 2 and lived among us.

All **Hail, Mary . . .**

With My Family

This Week . . .

In Chapter 5, "Jesus, the Son of God," your child learned that:

▶ God and his people made the Covenant with one another.

▶ The Covenant is the promise of God's love and mercy, and the promise of his people to love and serve God above all else.

▶ When Adam and Eve sinned and broke the Covenant, God promised to send someone to renew the Covenant.

▶ God fulfilled his promise by sending his Son, Jesus Christ, who became man and lived among us. Jesus Christ is true God and true man. He is the new and everlasting Covenant.

▶ The virtue of mercy helps us act with kindness toward others.

For more about related teachings of the Church, see the *Catechism of the Catholic Church*, 51–67 and 456–560, and the *United States Catholic Catechism for Adults*, pages 77–87.

■ Sharing God's Word

Read together Luke 2:1–14, about Jesus' birth. Or read the play about the Nativity on page 70. Emphasize that Jesus Christ is the Son of God. Jesus' birth is one of the most important signs that God always keeps his promise to love us.

■ Live as Disciples

The Christian home and family is a school of discipleship. Choose one of the following activities to do as a family, or design a similar activity of your own:

▶ Share ways that your family is already a living sign of God's love and kindness.

▶ Jesus told people repeatedly about God's love for them. Look around your home for something that reminds you of God's love. Talk about what it tells you about God's love.

■ Our Spiritual Journey

Devotion to Mary is a hallmark of Catholic living. Mary is an exemplar of holiness and hope and a witness to faith. She is the Mother of Jesus and our mother, too. Include a devotion to Mary, the Mother of God, in the spiritual journey of your family. In this chapter, your child prayed part of the Angelus. This prayer was traditionally prayed three times a day. Read and pray together the prayer on page 75. Pray the Hail Mary as a family each day.

For more ideas on ways your family can live as disciples of Jesus, visit **BeMyDisciples.com**

CHAPTER 6

Jesus, the Savior

? What would you give up to help a friend? Jesus told his friends,

"Love one another. You know how I have loved you. Love one another the same way. Remember, the greatest love you can show is to give up your life for your friends."

BASED ON JOHN 13:34; 15:13

? What are some ways that Jesus showed love for others?

Disciple Power

Sacrifice

You sacrifice when you give up something because you love someone. Jesus sacrificed his life for all people. Followers of Jesus make sacrifices out of love for God and for people.

The Church Follows **Jesus**

Saint Elizabeth of Hungary

Elizabeth was born many years ago. Her parents were the king and queen of the country called Hungary. Princess Elizabeth was very rich. She was also very generous. She loved Jesus very much. She followed Jesus' Commandment to love as he loved.

Elizabeth loved the people in her country. After her husband died, she gave up everything she had, out of her love for God and others.

Princess Elizabeth gave away her fancy clothes and jewels and money to help people. She shared her money with people who were poor. She gave food to people who were hungry. She cared for people who were sick and even had a hospital built to care for them.

Today we remember Princess Elizabeth as Saint Elizabeth of Hungary. We celebrate her feast on November 17.

? How did Saint Elizabeth show her love for Jesus and for the people of Hungary?

Saint Elizabeth shows us that loving God and loving people is not always easy. Sometimes we have to put the needs of others first. Sometimes we have to give up what we want and make a sacrifice.

Loving Sacrifices

To sacrifice is to give up something out of love. Read the sentences below. Decide which children are putting the needs of others first and choosing to sacrifice. Circle their names.

Manuel

My brother wants to change the TV station from my favorite channel to his favorite channel. I let him.

Doreen

My little sister wants to wear my bracelet. No way!

Linh

My mom is sick. Instead of playing after school, I'll come right home to help take care of my baby brother.

Write something you could sacrifice or give up out of love for someone else.

_____

_____

_____

God Sends the Savior

God promised to send his people a savior. A savior is a person who sets people free. God the Father sent his Son Jesus to be the Savior of the world. God sent Jesus to save people from their sins.

Read this Bible story. Saint Matthew tells us about the announcement that God would send the Savior.

One night when Joseph was sleeping, an angel brought him a message from God. The angel said to Joseph, "Mary, your wife, will give birth to a son. You are to name him, Jesus. He will save his people from their sins. All this will happen to fulfill God's promises."

BASED ON MATTHEW 1:20–23

When the child was born, Joseph named him Jesus. When Jesus grew up, he loved God and us so much he made a great sacrifice for us. Jesus died on the Cross to free us from our sins.

? How was Jesus our Savior?

Activity

The Name of Jesus

Look at this name:

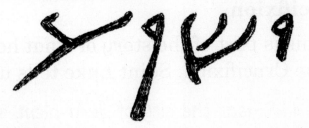

It is the name *Jesus*. It is written in the language Jesus spoke.

Do you know what the name *Jesus* means? Find out. Color the spaces marked with an X blue. Color spaces marked with a Y with other bright colors.

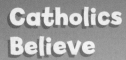

Catholics Believe

The Crucifix

The crucifix is a cross with an image of Jesus on it. The crucifix is a sign of God's love and mercy. Many families have a crucifix in their homes. Some Christians wear a crucifix on a chain around the neck to show their love for Jesus. There is a crucifix always placed near the altar in church.

Faith Focus
Why do we call Jesus Christ the Savior of all people?

Faith Words
Crucifixion
The Crucifixion is the Death of Jesus on a cross.

Jesus Died on the Cross

Jesus showed his love for his Father and for all people by freely dying on the Cross. Jesus' death on a cross is called the **Crucifixion**.

This is part of the story of what happened at the Crucifixion. Saint Luke tells us,

> On a hill near the city of Jerusalem, soldiers put Jesus to death on a cross. The name of the hill is Calvary. The sky became very dark. Jesus said, "Father, forgive them." Then Jesus died.

BASED ON LUKE 23:33–34, 44, 46

Jesus' Death on the Cross is also called the Sacrifice of the Cross. Jesus sacrificed his life to save and free us from sin and death. Through Jesus' Death on the Cross, God forgives us our sins.

? What does the Crucifixion mean?

Jesus' loving sacrifice has made us friends with God again. Because of Jesus' love, we can live forever with God in Heaven. The Bible says:

By his cross, Jesus forgave our sins. Now we can live forever with God.

BASED ON 1 PETER 2:24

Jesus is our Savior. Jesus is the Savior of the world!

? Why do we make sacrifices?

Activity

Praying to Jesus

Match the numbers with the letters. Fill in the missing letters. Discover a prayer to our Savior.

E = 1	U = 5	S = 9
H = 2	A = 6	F = 10
R = 3	K = 7	K = 11
O = 4	N = 8	G = 12

T_____ _____ _____ _____ Y_____ _____, J_____ _____ _____ _____ _____.
  2   6   8   7   4   5   1   9   5   9

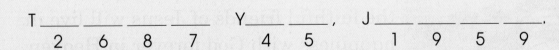

_____ _____ _____ _____ _____ _____ v i _____ _____ _____ _____!
 10   4   3   9   6   8   12   5   9

Jesus Is Raised to New Life

Something amazing happened three days after Jesus died and was buried in the tomb. Mary Magdalene and two other women disciples of Jesus went to the place where Jesus was buried. When they arrived there, the women saw that the body of Jesus was not there.

Two men dressed in bright white robes appeared to the women and said, "Jesus is not here. He has been raised." The women left the tomb and told the Apostles and others what happened. Peter and the others did not believe them. Peter rushed to the tomb to see for himself if what the women disciples said was true.

BASED ON LUKE 24:4, 6, 9, 11–12

Jesus rose from the dead to new life. We call this the **Resurrection**.

We too shall live after we die. All the faithful friends of Jesus will live in happiness with God forever in Heaven.

? Why is the Resurrection so important?

Jesus is the Savior of all people. He sacrificed his life out of love for his Father and for all people. The Holy Spirit invites you to share this Good News with everyone.

I Follow Jesus

Activity

Alleluia! Praise God!

Design this bookmark with colors and pictures that help you remember Jesus is the Savior of the world.

Save us, Savior of the world,
for by your Cross and Resurrection
you have set us free.

Alleluia!

MEMORIAL ACCLAMATION C, ROMAN MISSAL

My Faith Choice

Think of how you can tell others about the Good News of Jesus' saving love for all people. I will

_____

_____.

Pray, "Thank you, Jesus, for your sacrifice. Thank you for giving up your life to free us from sin. Amen."

TO HELP YOU REMEMBER

1. Jesus Christ is the Savior of the world.

2. Jesus sacrificed his life on the Cross to save all people from their sins.

3. God the Father raised his Son, Jesus, from death to new life.

Recall

Use the words in the box to complete the sentences.

Savior	Resurrection	Crucifixion

1. God the Father raising Jesus to new life is

   called the _____.

2. God the Father sent Jesus to be the

   _____.

3. Jesus' Death on a Cross is called the

   _____.

Circle yes or no for each sentence.

4. Jesus died on the Cross because he loves us. **Yes   No**

5. The Crucifixion means that Jesus was raised from the dead. **Yes   No**

6. The Resurrection is God's promise that we will live forever with him in Heaven. **Yes   No**

Reflect

Why is Jesus' Resurrection so important to us?

_____

_____.

Share — Share with a friend or classmate something that you sacrificed.

Praise God

Acclamations are prayers of praise. We pray acclamations to praise God for all the wonderful things he has done.

Leader
Saint John was with Jesus as he died on the Cross. Listen to this reading from John's Gospel.

Reader 1
On the first day of the week, Mary Magdala came to the tomb early in the morning, while it was still dark, and saw the stone removed from the tomb.

Reader 2
So she ran and went to Simon Peter and to the other disciple whom Jesus loved, and told them,

Reader 3
"They have taken the Lord from the tomb, and we don't know where they put him."

JOHN 20:1–2

The Gospel of the Lord.

All
Praise to you, Lord Jesus Christ.

Leader
Now let us proclaim the mystery of faith.

All
Save us, Savior of the world, for by your Cross and Resurrection you have set us free.

MEMORIAL ACCLAMATION C, ROMAN MISSAL

With My Family

This Week . . .

In Chapter 6, "Jesus, the Savior," your child learned:

▶ Salvation flows from God's initiative of love and mercy. God the Father sent his Son, Jesus, who freely chose to sacrifice his life on the Cross to free all people from sin.

▶ Three days after his Death and burial, Jesus rose from the dead to a new and glorified life. We call this event the Resurrection.

▶ We too shall live after we die. God invites us to live an eternal life of happiness.

▶ Jesus sacrificed his life for all people. Followers of Jesus make sacrifices out of love for God and for people.

For more about related teachings of the Church, see the *Catechism of the Catholic Church*, 422–451, 456–478, and 599–655, and the *United States Catholic Catechism for Adults*, pages 91–98.

■ Sharing God's Word

Read together the Bible story about Jesus' dying on the Cross and his rising from the dead. Emphasize that the Death and Resurrection of Jesus are the greatest signs of God's love for people.

■ Living as Disciples

The Christian home and family is a school of discipleship. Choose one of the following activities to do as a family, or design a similar activity of your own:

▶ The crucifix reminds us of God's love for us. Display a crucifix in your home. Gather around it and talk about God's love for your family.

▶ Help your child practice making sacrifices. Offer him or her opportunities to choose others over him- or herself. For example, if your child receives an allowance, suggest ways he or she can give a portion to help the hungry.

■ Our Spiritual Journey

The Sacrifice of the Cross is the greatest expression of God's love for people. Christians are people of sacrifice. In this chapter, your child learned to pray a Memorial Acclamation used at Mass. Read and pray together the prayer on page 86. Pray the acclamation: *Save us, Savior of the world, for by your Cross and Resurrection you have set us free* (Memorial Acclamation C, Roman Missal).

For more ideas on ways your family can live as disciples of Jesus, visit **BeMyDisciples.com**

CHAPTER 7

The Holy Spirit

? What is the best gift someone ever gave you?

Saint Paul tells us,

God loves you very much. God sends you the Holy Spirit. The Holy Spirit gives special spiritual gifts to each person. The Holy Spirit wants us to use our gifts to help and serve others.   BASED ON 1 CORINTHIANS 12:4–11

? What special gifts do you have that help and serve others?

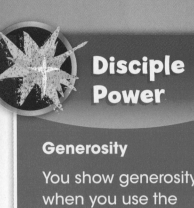

Disciple Power

Generosity

You show generosity when you use the gifts you receive from God to help others.

Kids' Kitchen

We all receive blessings and gifts from the Holy Spirit. Even second graders get these gifts! One of these gifts is the gift of generosity.

Sagen was in second grade when she saw that some children ate free lunches at school. She wondered, "What do they do during the summer? Do they get to eat lunch every day? How can I help?"

Sagen went to Sam, who was in charge of the soup kitchen in her parish. Sam helped Sagen organize her own kitchen for kids. She called it Kids' Kitchen.

The word spread about Kids' Kitchen. Soon, ten parishes were donating food. Sagen and her friends were serving lunch to over 600 children. Those children also took food home to their families.

Someone asked Sagen why she started Kids' Kitchen. "To help people," she said. "That's what I hear in church on Sunday."

? Why did Sagen start Kids' Kitchen?

Sagen saw what was needed. Hungry children needed lunch in the summertime. So Sagen generously used her gifts to meet the need.

Activity

Gifts Help the Need

Look at each picture below. Write what you think is needed in each. Then think of your gifts. Write how you could be generous with your gifts to meet the need.

1. What is needed?

_____

Here is how I can use my gifts to meet the need.

_____

2. What is needed?

_____

Here is how I can use my gifts to meet the need.

_____

3. What is needed?

_____

Here is how I can use my gifts to meet the need.

_____

Faith Focus
What does the New Testament tell us about the Holy Spirit?

Faith Words
Ascension
The Ascension is the return of the Risen Jesus to his Father in Heaven after the Resurrection.

The Gift of the Holy Spirit

After the Resurrection, Jesus made a special promise to his disciples. He said,

I am sending the promise of my Father to you. It is the gift of the Holy Spirit.

BASED ON LUKE 24:49

The Holy Spirit is the Third Person of the Holy Trinity.

Jesus made this promise after the Resurrection, just before he returned to his Father in Heaven. We call the return of the Risen Jesus to his Father in Heaven the **Ascension**.

❓ What did Jesus promise his disciples?

 Activity

A Promise of Love

Jesus' promise filled the disciples with great joy. Use the words in the box. Fill in the crossword puzzle about the promise of love.

Ascension	Jesus	Spirit
Gift	Heaven	Resurrection

Catholics Believe

Gifts of the Holy Spirit

The Holy Spirit blesses us with spiritual gifts. These gifts help us to follow Jesus and to live as children of God.

Down

1. Jesus made his promise after the _____.

4. The Holy _____ is the Third Person of the Holy Trinity.

Across

2. The return of the Risen Jesus to the Father is called the _____.

3. _____ made a special promise to his disciples.

5. Jesus promised a special _____.

6. Jesus returned to his Father in _____.

Faith Focus
How is the Holy Spirit
always with us?

Pentecost

The promise of the Holy Spirit came true fifty days after the Ascension. The day that the Holy Spirit came to the Apostles is called **Pentecost**. Saint Luke tells us that after Jesus returned to his Father, the disciples and Mary, the mother of Jesus, were praying together in a room.

> And suddenly there came from the sky a noise like a strong driving wind, and it filled the entire house in which they were. Then there appeared to them tongues as of fire, which parted and came to rest on each one of them. And they were all filled with the holy Spirit . . . .
>
> ACTS OF THE APOSTLES 2:1–4

Peter and the disciples then left the house. They went to tell others about Jesus.

Each year, fifty days after Easter, we remember and celebrate Pentecost. We celebrate the wonderful gift of the Holy Spirit.

We first receive the gift of the Holy Spirit at Baptism. He gives us special gifts to live as followers of Jesus. The Holy Spirit helps us tell others about Jesus as Peter did.

? What is one thing you want to tell someone about Jesus?

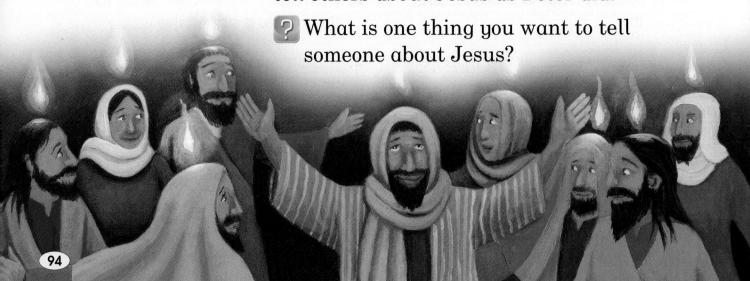

The Holy Spirit

The circle maze has five paths that form five sentences about the Holy Spirit. The name *Holy Spirit* in the center is the first word of each sentence. Find a path from the center to the outside row. The words will be in order forming a sentence. Write each sentence on a line.

THE HOLY SPIRIT . . .

1. _____

2. _____

3. _____

4. _____

5. _____

Faith-Filled People

Saint Luke

Luke sometimes traveled from place to place with Saint Paul. Together they preached the Gospel. They told people all about Jesus. Saint Luke is one of the four Evangelists, or "tellers of the Gospel."

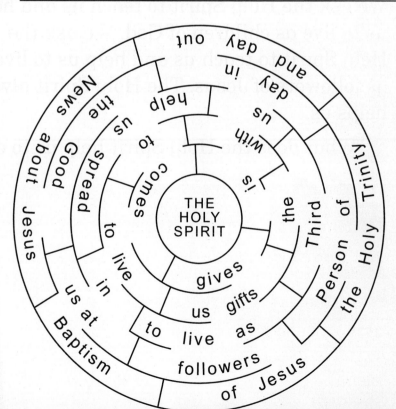

The Holy Spirit Is Always with Us

The Holy Spirit is the Helper and Teacher Jesus sent to us. The Holy Spirit helps us to believe and trust in God the Father and in Jesus Christ.

The Holy Spirit helps and teaches us to pray. He helps us to pray the way Jesus taught us. We pray to God our Father. We tell God the Father what is in our thoughts and in our hearts.

The Holy Spirit helps us to pray even when we do not know what to say. The Bible tells us,

When we do not have the right words to pray, the Holy Spirit prays for us in ways more powerful than words.

BASED ON ROMANS 8:26

So, we ask the Holy Spirit to help us pray. We ask the Holy Spirit to teach us and help us to live as children of God. We ask the Holy Spirit to teach us and help us to live as followers of Jesus. The Holy Spirit always helps us.

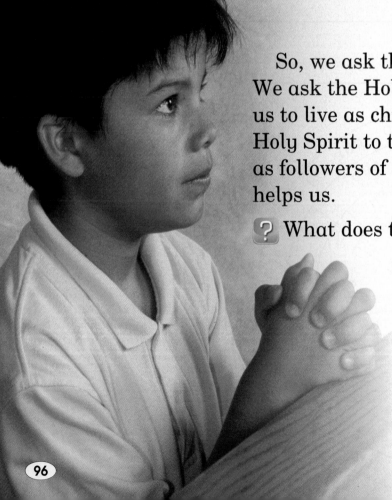 **?** What does the Holy Spirit help us to do?

The Holy Spirit gives you gifts. These gifts are sometimes called talents. Talents help us to do good things. These gifts help you to know God's love. Generosity helps you use those gifts to help others.

I Follow Jesus

Activity

Sharing the Gift of God's Love

A flame of fire is one symbol the Church uses for the Holy Spirit. Think of your talents. In the flame, show how you use one talent to help others.

My Faith Choice

This week, I will be generous. I will use my talents. I will share the gift of God's love with other people. I will

_____

_____.

Pray, "Thank the Holy Spirit for helping you to use your talents to help others. Amen."

1. Before he returned to his Father in Heaven, Jesus promised that the Father would send the Holy Spirit.

2. The Holy Spirit came to the disciples on Pentecost.

3. The Holy Spirit is our Helper and Teacher.

Chapter Review

Recall

Match each word with its correct meaning.

	Words		Meanings
_____ **1.**	Pentecost	**a.**	One who asked the Father to send the Holy Spirit
_____ **2.**	Ascension	**b.**	the day the work of the Church began
_____ **3.**	Jesus	**c.**	Third Person of the Holy Trinity
_____ **4.**	Holy Spirit	**d.**	the return of the Risen Jesus to his Father in Heaven

Reflect

Reflect and then complete each of the following statements.

🔼 I think a good title for the Holy Spirit would be

_____

_____.

🔼 I believe the Holy Spirit can help me

_____

_____.

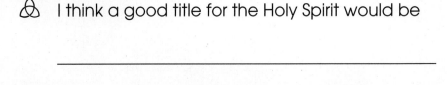

Share   Share your responses with the class to make a prayer list for the ways the Holy Spirit can help you and your classmates.

Come, Holy Spirit

Pray this prayer to the Holy Spirit.

Leader   Let us pray to the Holy Spirit.

All   **Come, Holy Spirit.**

Group 1   Fill the hearts of your faithful.

All   **Come, Holy Spirit.**

Group 2   Kindle in us the fire of your love.

All   **Come, Holy Spirit.**

Group 3   Send forth your Spirit and we shall be created.

All   **Come, Holy Spirit.**

Group 1   Enter our hearts that we may love.

All   **Come, Holy Spirit.**

Group 2   Guide our minds that we may understand your teaching.

All   **Come, Holy Spirit.**

Group 3   Inspire our imaginations that we may know your presence.

All   **Come, Holy Spirit, renew the face of the Earth. Amen.**

With My Family

This Week . . .

In Chapter 7, "The Holy Spirit," your child learned:

- The Holy Spirit is the Third Person of the Holy Trinity.
- The Father and the Son sent the Holy Spirit to be our helper and teacher.
- The Holy Spirit is the source of all the Church does.
- The Holy Spirit helps the whole Church to learn and to live what Jesus taught.
- The Holy Spirit helps all the baptized to pray and to live as children of God and followers of Christ.
- When we practice the virtue of generosity, we show that we are thankful for the gifts we receive from God.

For more about related teachings of the Church, see the *Catechism of the Catholic Church,* 687–741, and the *United States Catholic Catechism for Adults,* pages 102–108.

Sharing God's Word

Read together Acts of the Apostles 2:1–6 about the coming of the Holy Spirit on Pentecost. Or read the adaptation of the story on page 94. Emphasize that the Holy Spirit came to the disciples on Pentecost to help them do the work that Jesus gave them, namely, to tell the world about Jesus and make disciples of people. Share that the Holy Spirit is always with your family to teach and help you to do the same.

Living as Disciples

The Christian home and family is a school of discipleship. Choose one of the following activities to do as a family, or design a similar activity of your own:

- Pray to the Holy Spirit before meals or bedtime this week. Use the prayer on page 98. Talk about how your family can tell others about Jesus.

- Help your child grow in generosity. Before they will receive gifts, such as birthday gifts, have him or her give something else away. After giving, remind your child that disciples are generous with others.

Our Spiritual Journey

Almsgiving is sharing our material and spiritual blessings because of our love for God and for people. Almsgiving is an expression of generosity which flows from one's gratitude to God. Pray the refrain, "Come, Holy Spirit, come." Praise and thank God, both in words and deeds, for his blessings.

For more ideas on ways your family can live as disciples of Jesus, visit **BeMyDisciples.com**

CHAPTER 8

The Church

? To which communities do you belong?

The Church is a community. Saint Luke tells us,

> The followers of Jesus shared everything with one another. They prayed and broke bread together. They praised God together. They learned more about what Jesus taught. Other people saw how the followers of Jesus loved one another. Every day God helped more and more people join the Church.

BASED ON ACTS OF THE APOSTLES 2:42–47

? What can you can do with other members of the Church?

Goodness

Goodness is a sign that we are living our Baptism. When we are good to people, we show that we know they are children of God. When we are good to people, we honor God.

Father Augustus Tolton

Augustus' family was very poor. He and his family came from Africa. They were brought to America to be slaves. But the family escaped from slavery.

They lived at a time when black children were not allowed to go to the same school as other children. Augustus' mother did not give up and found a school he could attend. He grew up knowing God wanted him to become a priest.

Augustus became the first black priest in the United States of America. Father Augustus became the pastor of a parish and school.

Priests do special work in the Church. They lead the members of the Church in worship. Priests help people understand the Word of God.

❓ What kinds of work does the pastor do with the people of your parish?

Father Tolton was the pastor of a special community called a parish. A pastor is a priest who helps and leads the people of a parish community.

The Parish Community

Write the name of your pastor.

The pastor of my parish is

_____

Parish is a very old word. It comes from a word that means "being close together." Write the name of your parish community.

The name of my parish is

_____

Today, people in a parish are close together in many ways. They worship, pray, and celebrate together. They also share in giving service to help others.

Write about a favorite way you like to be together with your parish community.

_____

_____

_____

Names for the Church

God sent Jesus to all people. Jesus told the Apostles to invite all people to become his followers. Jesus said,

"[M]ake disciples of all nations, baptizing them . . . teaching them to observe all that I have commanded you."

MATTHEW 28:19–20

The Holy Spirit invites all people from every race and nation to become disciples of Jesus. The Church is the new People of God.

We are **Catholics**. We belong to the Catholic Church. We become members of the Church at Baptism. God's people in the Catholic Church share the same faith and Sacraments.

? What do members of the Catholic Church share?

We are led by the Pope and the bishops. The Pope and the bishops take the place of the Apostles in the Church today.

? Who is the Pope and how does he help us?

Activity

Praying for Church Leaders

Find out the name of your bishop or archbishop. Write a prayer for him. Tell him you are praying for him.

_____

_____

_____

_____

_____

_____

_____

_____

_____

Pope Francis

Faith Words
▶ **Body of Christ**
The Church is the Body of Christ. Jesus Christ is the Head of the Church. All the baptized are members of the Church.

The Body of Christ

Saint Paul describes the Church as the **Body of Christ.** He wrote,

Our body has many parts, but it is still one body. We have been baptized into one body.

BASED ON 1 CORINTHIANS 12:12–13

The image of the Body of Christ helps us to understand what the Church is like. The Church is the one Body of Christ. Jesus is the Head. All the baptized are the Body.

All the parts of our body make up one body. Our eyes are different from our ears. Our brain is different from our heart.

Every part of our body has something different and important to do. All the members of the Church have something different and important to do.

? How does the image of the Body of Christ help us to understand what the Church is like?

Clothing Donations

As the Church, we are joined with Jesus, The Holy Spirit gives all members of the Church the grace to live as followers of Jesus.

? What is one way you live as a follower of Jesus?

Activity

Followers of Jesus

Look at each picture. Next to the number for each picture, write how the people are living as followers of Jesus. Next to the number 3, write how you live as a follower of Jesus.

1._____.

2._____.

3._____

_____

_____.

Faith Words
Communion of Saints
The Church is the
Communion of Saints.
The Church is the
unity of all the faithful
followers of Jesus on
Earth and those in
Heaven.

The Communion of Saints

The Church is called the People of God and the Body of Christ. Another name for the Church is the **Communion of Saints,** all the faithful People of God. The Church, the Communion of Saints, includes all the faithful followers of Jesus who live on Earth and those in Heaven.

The Church names some people who have died "saints." These Saints live in Heaven. They join with Mary and the angels and praise God with their whole hearts.

Mary is the greatest Saint. She is the Mother of God. Jesus told us that Mary is our mother. Mary is the Mother of the Church.

The Church honors Mary and the other Saints in many ways. We pray to Mary and the Saints. We have images of Mary and the other Saints to help us love God and other people with our whole heart.

[?] Who is your favorite Saint? Why?

ELIZABETH ANN SETON

ELIZABETH OF PORTUGAL

ANDRÉ BESSETTE

You are a member of the Body of Christ, the Church. You are a child of God. You can be good to others by helping them.

I Follow Jesus

Activity

Sharing your Faith

Think of how the Holy Spirit helps you live as a member of the Church. Write or draw something you can do with others in the Church.

My Faith choice

This week, I will show goodness by working together with my Church to help others. I will

_____

_____.

Pray, "Saints of God, pray for me and my family. Amen."

Chapter Review

Recall

Color the box next to the sentences that are true.

☐ Jesus gave us the Church.

☐ The Holy Spirit invites all people to become disciples of Jesus.

☐ Jesus Christ is the Head of the Church.

☐ Augustus Tolton is the greatest Saint of the Church.

Use the best word in the box to complete each sentence.

Catholic	Mary	Church	Body of Christ

1. The _____ is the People of God.

2. Saint Paul tells us that the Church is the

   _____ _____ _____.

3. _____ is the Mother of God.

Reflect
Why is the Church the Communion of Saints?

_____

_____

_____

Share   Share with a classmate how you are an important part of the Body of Christ.

A Litany of Saints

A litany is one kind of prayer the Church prays. When we pray a litany, we repeat one part over and over again. Pray the litany with your class.

Leader   Holy Mary, Mother of God

All   **pray for us.**

Leader   Saint Joseph

All   **pray for us.**

Leader   Saint Martin de Porres

All   **pray for us.**

Leader   Saint Elizabeth of Hungary

All   **pray for us.**

Leader   Saint Patrick

All   **pray for us.**

Leader   All holy men and women

All   **pray for us.**

Leader   Now, as one body, let us join in prayer to the Saints.

All   **Holy Saints, please pray for me in your gentle way. Help me learn how I should be. Watch over me each day. Amen.**

With My Family

This Week . . .

In Chapter 8, "The Church," your child learned:

▶ The Church is the community of the faithful followers of Jesus.

▶ The Church is the People of God, the Body of Christ, and the Communion of Saints. Mary is the greatest Saint and Mother of the Church.

▶ All of the baptized have important roles in the work of the Church.

▶ As members of the Church, we are one in Christ. With the Holy Spirit, we can show goodness to one another. We support and care for and show respect for one another as Jesus taught.

For more about related teachings of the Church, see the *Catechism of the Catholic Church*, 751–776, 781–801, and 874–993, and the *United States Catholic Catechism for Adults*, pages 143–147.

■ Sharing God's Word

Read together Matthew 28:19–20, about Jesus giving the Apostles the mission to make disciples of all people. Or read the adaptation of the passage on page 104. This mission is called evangelization. It is the primary work of the Church. Emphasize that the Church today continues the work Jesus gave to the first disciples.

■ Living as Disciples

The Christian home and family is a school of discipleship. Choose one of the following activities to do as a family, or design a similar activity of your own:

▶ Talk about the many ways your family is already taking part in the work of the Church.

▶ Goodness is one of the twelve Fruits of the Holy Spirit. When we cooperate with the Holy Spirit, we are good to others. As a family, become more involved in your parish's outreach ministries to show the goodness of God to others. Look to your family's special gifts and then decide on ways you can be good to others.

■ Our Spiritual Journey

Joined to Christ and all the members of Church at Baptism, we are strengthened and made stronger with Christ and with all the Saints in the celebration and reception of the Eucharist. Take part in the Eucharist frequently. Your child prayed part of the Litany of the Saints. Read and pray together the prayer on page 111. Add the names of your favorite and/or patron Saints. After each name, have all respond, "Pray for us."

For more ideas on ways your family can live as disciples of Jesus, visit **BeMyDisciples.com**

Caring for All

Mr. Moody was the head of a school for one hundred and twenty Hmong and Karen refugee children. He was proud of his students. They were learning new things, especially, how to speak and read English.

Soon, the school year would end. Mr. Moody wanted his students to keep reading and learning English over the summer. But he knew they did not have the money to buy books. Mr. Moody started to worry.

Sally Curran lived next door to Mr. Moody. When she heard about his worry, she decided to talk to her teacher and friends about it at her school, St. Cecilia's. Sally told her class about Mr. Moody's problem. She said that she wished they could help.

The class thought and thought and then decided. They asked every student in St. Cecilia's school to donate new or gently used books for Mr. Moody's students. They collected lots of books. On the last day of school, the students from St. Cecilia's delivered them to the Hmong and Karen refugee children. Each child received six books. Mr. Moody smiled!

WE ARE UNITED WITH OTHERS

We are all God's children. We are one human family. We must care for people of all nations just as we care for those closest to us.

Making Connections

Blessed Pope John Paul II said, "We are all really responsible for all." That means we are to care about all people, not just those close to us. No matter our differences, we are one human family called to care for one another.

with Language Arts

Imagine you are a student at St. Cecilia's school. Write a letter to one of the Hmong or Karen students at Mr. Moody's school. Invite the student to be your pen pal. Then tell your pen pal about your favorite book. Be sure to include the title and author of the book. Also, tell why you like it so much.

with Math and Science

The children at St. Cecilia's collected enough books for each child at Mr. Moody's school to have six books. There are 120 Hmong and Karen students. How many books did the St. Cecilia students collect? Each student at St. Cecilia's gave three books. How many St. Cecilia students are there?

with Creative Arts

A quilt is made of many different parts. All the parts make a quilt. A quilt is a way to show how people are different but all part of God's family. Create a paper solidarity quilt. Decide on a theme. Everyone creates a drawing on an 8" x 8" square paper "patch." Put the "patches" together to form a "quilt."

Faith Action

Decide to be more welcoming to classmates who may be left out by others. I will show that we are all one as part of God's family by _____

_____

_____.

Unit 2 Review

A. Choose the Best Word

Fill in the blanks to complete each of the sentences.
Use the words from the word bank.

Pentecost	Covenant	People of God
Baptism	crucifixion	

1. God made a solemn _____ with his people.

2. We call Jesus' dying on the Cross the _____.

3. God sent the Holy Spirit on the day of _____.

4. We first receive the Holy Spirit in the Sacrament

   of _____.

5. The Church is also called the _____.

B. Show What You Know

Match the items in Column A with those in Column B.

Column A

____ 1. Communion of Saints

____ 2. the faithful

____ 3. Resurrection

____ 4. Ascension

____ 5. mercy

Column B

A. The virtue that helps us to act with kindness toward others no matter what

B. God the Father raising Jesus from the dead to new life

C. The unity of all the faithful followers of Jesus on Earth and those who have died

D. What members of the Church are called

E. What we call the return of the Risen Jesus to his Father in Heaven

C. Connect with Scripture

What was your favorite story about Jesus in this unit?
Draw something that happened in the story.
Tell your class about it.

D. Be a Disciple

1. *What Saint or holy person did you enjoy hearing about in this unit? Write the name here. Tell your class what this person did to follow Jesus.*

_____

_____

2. *What can you do to be a good disciple of Jesus?*

_____

_____

Zacchaeus and Jesus

A tiny man named Zacchaeus lived in the town of Jericho. He collected money from the town's people to give to the rulers.

One day Jesus came to Jericho. Tiny Zacchaeus could not see him, so he quickly climbed a tree. Just then, Jesus walked by. "Zacchaeus," Jesus shouted, "come down! I want to stay with you."

Zacchaeus hopped down and welcomed Jesus. Jesus taught him to treat people fairly. Zacchaeus said, "I will give half of all I own to the poor."

Jesus smiled and said, "You are part of God's family."

BASED ON LUKE 19:1–10

What I Know

What is something you already know about these faith concepts?

Baptism

_____

_____

Sin

_____

_____

Reconciliation

_____

_____

*Put an **X** next to the faith words you know. Put a **?** next to the faith words you need to learn more about.*

_____ worship   _____ grace   _____ Confirmation

_____ Sacraments   _____ penance   _____ Spiritual Gifts

What do you know about God's promises to his people in the Bible?

_____

A Question I Have

What question would you like to ask about forgiveness?

_____

_____

CHAPTER 9

We Celebrate God's Love

❓ What is your favorite celebration?

The Holy Family celebrated God's love together. Listen to one of their prayers.

> Shout joyfully to the LORD,
> 　　all you lands;
> 　worship the LORD with cries
> 　　of gladness;
> come before him with joyful song.
>
> PSALM 100:1–2

❓ What are some things you say or do when you celebrate God's love with your school or parish family?

Disciple Power

Piety

Piety is a Gift of the Holy Spirit. Piety is the love we have for God. That love makes us want to worship and give God thanks and praise.

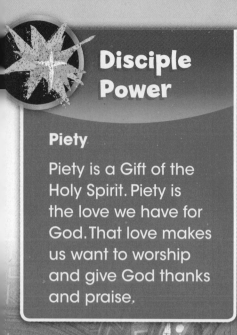

Blessed John XXIII

Pope John XXIII wanted all Catholics to celebrate God's love in the Mass. He wanted everyone to love and take part in the Mass.

Many years ago, Pope John XXIII called a meeting of all the bishops in the world. They worked together to make changes to some of the ways we celebrate the Mass.

The bishops worked together to make sure everyone could understand the words. They wanted to make sure that everyone could worship God at Mass in their own language.

Today we continue to celebrate Mass with a greater love for God. The words and actions we say and do at Mass help us worship God with thanks and praise.

❓ Which words and actions at Mass do you enjoy?

Using words and actions at Mass help us worship God. The words and actions that we say and do with each other is important too. They help us to honor God and others.

? What are some words and actions that you say or do to honor God and others?

Activity

The Right Words

For each picture below decide which words in the word bubbles will help. Draw a line from the word bubble to the picture.

I will help.

I am sorry.

Let's say grace.

Do it yourself.

Faith Focus
What do the words
and actions of Jesus
teach us?

We Worship God

Jesus used words and actions to show God's love for us. One time, a man named Jairus came to Jesus.

Jairus was a religious leader who had great faith in God. Jairus asked Jesus to help his daughter who was very sick. Read what happened next:

Jesus and his disciples followed Jairus to his house. When they arrived there, Jesus saw the family and neighbors weeping. He then took Jairus, his wife and the disciples and entered the house and went over to the daughter of Jairus. Jesus took her by the hand and said, "Little girl, I say to you, arise!" The girl got up immediately and walked around. And Jesus told her parents to give her something to eat.

BASED ON MARK 5:22–24, 38, 41–42

People listened carefully to what Jesus said. They watched carefully everything Jesus did. After this, more people came to believe in Jesus and to place their trust in him.

The words and actions of Jesus helped the people believe that Jesus is the Son of God. The words and actions of Jesus helped them understand how much God loves us.

 What do Jesus' words and actions show us?

Activity

Jesus' Words and Actions

With your classmates, create a skit that shows the words and actions of Jesus in this Gospel story. In your skit, show how Jesus helped others believe that he is the Son of God. Draw a scene from your skit.

Faith Words

worship
Worship means to honor and love God above all else.

Sacraments
The Sacraments are the seven signs of God's love for us that Jesus gave the Church. We share in God's love when we celebrate the Sacraments.

We Praise God

God loves us very much. One way we show our love for God is to **worship** him. To worship God means to honor and love God above all else.

The Church uses words and actions to worship God. They tell God we believe in him, hope in him, and love him.

All the words and actions we use in worship show that God is sharing his love with us. We use them to celebrate the **Sacraments**. The Sacraments help us to give thanks and praise to God for all he has done for us.

Jesus gave the Church the Seven Sacraments as a special way to worship God. Each Sacrament is a sign of God's love for us.

Jesus is present with us when we celebrate the Sacraments. The Holy Spirit helps us to celebrate the Sacraments.

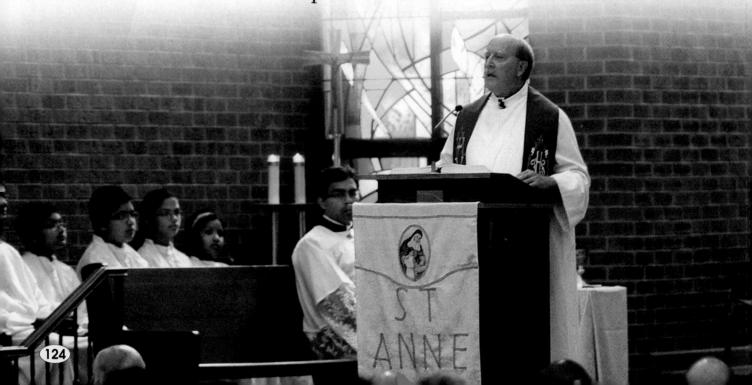

We worship God in the Sacraments. We listen to God. We honor and praise God. We pray aloud and we sing. We stand and sit and walk in procession.

Sometimes water is poured over us. Sometimes we are marked with oil. We offer and share bread and wine. We bless and receive blessings. We make promises.

? Why do we worship God? How do we worship him?

Activity

We Worship

Which of these pictures do you recognize as celebrations of the Church? Write what you see happening in each picture.

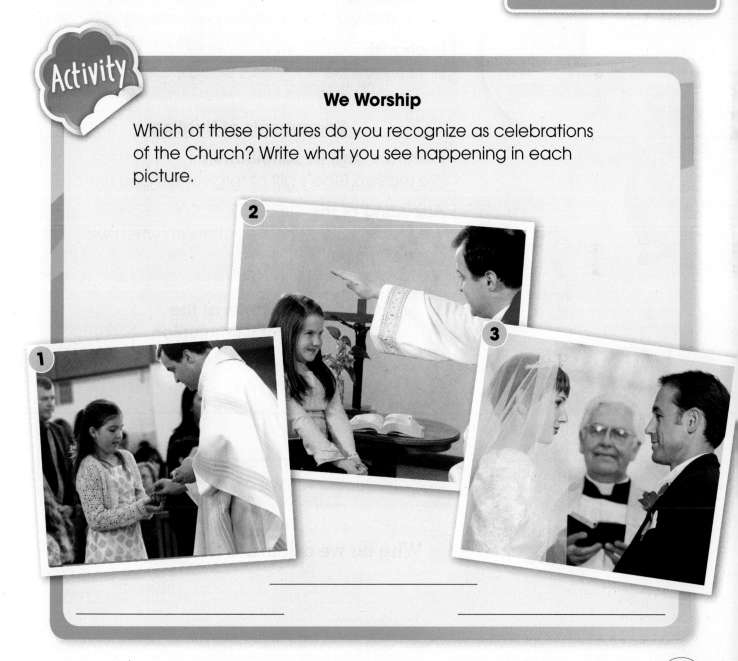

_____

_____   _____

The Seven Sacraments

The Sacraments are seven signs of God's love for us. When we celebrate the Sacraments, we share in God's love. The Sacraments are divided into three groups.

Sacraments of Christian Initiation

Baptism
We are joined to Jesus and become a part of his Church.

Confirmation
The Holy Spirit helps us to live as children of God.

Eucharist
We receive the Body and Blood of Jesus.

Sacraments of Healing

Penance and Reconciliation
We receive God's gift of forgiveness and mercy.

Anointing of the Sick
We receive God's healing strength when we are sick or dying.

Sacraments at the Service of Communion

Holy Orders
A baptized man is called by God to serve the Church as a bishop, priest, or deacon.

Matrimony
A baptized man and a baptized woman make a lifelong promise to love and respect each other.

Why do we celebrate the Sacraments?

The words and actions of the Sacraments are signs of God's love. Your words and actions can help people believe and trust in God's love. The Holy Spirit's gift of piety helps you want to be a sign of God's love.

I Follow Jesus

Activity

Praying with Actions

You can use many different actions when you pray. Finish each line of the prayer. Pray your prayer with the actions.

With hands outstretched,
I ask you, God, for

_____.

With hands folded,
I praise you, God, for

_____.

With head bowed,
I thank you, God, for

_____.

With hands raised high,
I show my love for you, O God! Amen.

My Faith Choice

This week, I will pray using both words and actions.

I will say my prayer

☐ in the morning.   ☐ after school.

☐ at dinnertime.   ☐ at bedtime.

Pray, "O Holy Spirit, let all my words and actions give praise and glory to God. Amen."

1. We worship God by using words and actions.

2. We worship God when we celebrate the Sacraments.

3. The Holy Spirit helps us to celebrate the Sacraments and worship God.

Chapter Review

Recall

Complete the sentences, using the words below.

Sacraments   love   actions   Seven

1. The words and actions of Jesus helped people

   to know God's _____.

2. We share in God's love when we celebrate the

   _____.

3. The Church uses words and _____
   to worship God.

4. Jesus gave the Church _____
   Sacraments.

Reflect

What are the ways that you can share in God's love?

_____

_____

_____

_____

Share   Share with your class how the Sacraments you have received have helped you.

We Bless the Lord

God has blessed us in many ways. We can offer God our thanks and bless his name in word and action.

Leader The Bible tells us to call upon the Lord with blessing.

Bless the Lord at all times.
Praise God forever.

BASED ON PSALM 34:2

Group 1 We bless your name and praise you, God, with this our grateful prayer.

Group 2 We bless you for the gifts of joy and laughter that we share.

Group 1 We bless you for Lord Jesus, his piety and care,

Group 2 And for his life and Cross that saved all people everywhere.

Group 1 We bless you for the words he spoke and all his actions, too.

Group 2 We bless you for the Sacraments, that help us love like you.

Group 1 We bless you for your constant love that's with us all our days.

Group 2 We bless you, God, and offer you our worship, thanks, and praise.

All **Amen.**

With My Family

This Week . . .

In Chapter 9, "We Celebrate God's Love," your child learned:

▶ The Church comes together to worship God.

▶ The words and actions of Jesus helped people come to believe in God and in his love for us.

▶ Through the celebration of the Sacraments, we worship God, and we are made sharers in the life and love of God.

▶ The Church uses special words and actions to celebrate the Sacraments.

▶ The virtue of piety, a special gift of the Holy Spirit, strengthens our desire to worship God.

For more about related teachings of the Church, see the *Catechism of the Catholic Church* 1066–1186, and the *United States Catholic Catechism for Adults,* pages 168–169 and 295–298.

■ Sharing God's Word

Read together Mark 5:41–42, Jesus healing the daughter of Jairus. Or read the adaptation of the story on page 122. Emphasize that Jesus healed people to show them God's love. Name and talk about some of the words and actions of your family that are signs of God's love.

■ Living as Disciples

The Christian home and family is a school of discipleship. Choose one of the following activities to do as a family, or design a similar activity of your own:

▶ Talk about the Sacraments that each family member has received. What words and actions do you remember from the celebration of each Sacrament? Discuss the meanings of those words and actions.

▶ Body language and gestures help us pray. This week hold hands when you pray as a family. Remember that you all belong to God's family as well as your family.

■ Our Spiritual Journey

Our spiritual journey is marked by signposts. The celebration of and participation in the Sacraments is vital and essential to the Christian life, in particular, participation in Mass and frequent reception of Holy Communion. Help your children learn to pray silently after Holy Communion, thanking God for his blessings in their own words. As a family say the prayer on page 129.

For more ideas on ways your family can live as disciples of Jesus, visit **BeMyDisciples.com**

CHAPTER 10

Our Church Welcomes Us

? Who are your friends? How did you become friends?

Saint Paul wrote many letters to Jesus' followers. Listen to what he wrote in this letter,

You have been baptized in Christ.
It does not matter where you come from.
It does not matter whether you are a
boy or a girl, or a man or a woman. By
Baptism you are all friends of Jesus.

BASED ON GALATIANS 3:26–28

? How do you show others that you are a friend and follower of Jesus?

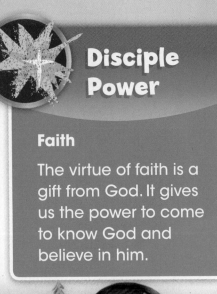

Disciple Power

Faith

The virtue of faith is a gift from God. It gives us the power to come to know God and believe in him.

The Church Follows **Jesus**

Saint Kateri

Kateri Tekakwitha was the daughter of a Native American Mohawk warrior chief. When Kateri was only four years old, her parents died from a terrible sickness. The same sickness left Kateri almost blind and with marks on her face.

One day, a priest visited her village. He told everyone that they could become followers of Jesus.

Kateri learned more and more about Jesus. Then she said she wanted to be baptized. She became a follower of Jesus. She became a member of the Church.

Kateri prayed to God every day. She thanked God for her faith. She helped people in need. Even when others treated her badly, she was always thankful for her Baptism and her faith.

? How did Kateri show her faith in God?

Kateri helped many other Native Americans become part of the Catholic Church. She showed them how to be followers of Jesus.

? What are the ways that you show your faith in God?

Activity

PEACE BE WITH YOU

Learn this Mohawk greeting. Greet others with peace, like Jesus asked his followers to greet people.

She:kon (Say go)

Skennon ko:wa (Sken in go wah).

Hello, great peace be with you!

Now write your own greeting of peace. Share it with your class.

_____

_____

_____

_____

_____

_____

Faith Words

Baptism
Baptism is the Sacrament that joins us to Christ and makes us members of the Church. We receive the gift of the Holy Spirit and become adopted sons and daughters of God.

deacon
A deacon is a baptized man blessed in the Sacrament of Holy Orders to serve the Church and to assist bishops and priests.

grace
Grace is the gift of God sharing his life with us and helping us live as his children.

Sacrament of Baptism

You learned about the Sacraments in the last chapter. Three Sacraments make us followers of Jesus. Celebrating the Sacraments of **Baptism**, Confirmation, and Eucharist joins us to Christ and makes us members of the Church. These three Sacraments are called Sacraments of Christian Initiation.

Baptism is the first Sacrament we celebrate. At the beginning of the celebration of Baptism, the priest or **deacon** asks the parents, "What do you ask of God for your child?" The parents answer, "Baptism" or "Faith."

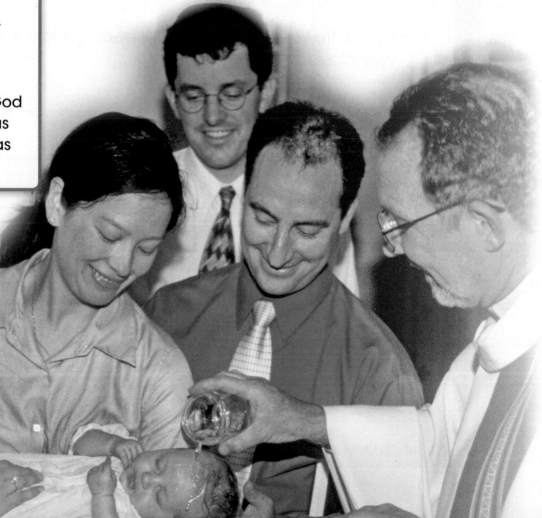

This is what happens to us at our Baptism. We are joined to Christ. We celebrate that we are followers of Jesus. We are welcomed into the Church.

We are given the gift of the Holy Spirit. We are given a special gift called sanctifying **grace**. God shares his life with us. We are called to live a holy life.

We become adopted sons and daughters of God. We are called to love God and our neighbor as Jesus taught.

 What does Baptism call us to do?

Catholics Believe

Baptismal Candle

At Baptism, we receive a lighted candle. The baptismal candle is lighted from the Easter candle. Each of us is given the lighted baptismal candle to remind us that we are to live our faith every day.

Activity

Living Our Baptism

Look at the pictures. The children are showing love for God and neighbor. Write a title for each picture. Talk with a partner about what you write.

_____   _____

_____   _____

Welcome to the Church

The Bible tells us about the Baptism of a man named Cornelius and his family.

Cornelius was a soldier in the Roman army. One day he asked Peter the Apostle to tell him about Jesus.

Peter told him all about how Jesus showed his love for God and for us. He told Cornelius about how Jesus died on the cross for all people. Then he told him that Jesus rose from the dead on the third day.

Peter invited Cornelius and his family to believe in Jesus. He said, "All who have faith in Jesus will receive forgiveness of sins." Cornelius and his family felt the Holy Spirit fill them. They believed and had faith. Peter then baptized them all.

BASED ON ACTS OF THE APOSTLES 10:30–48

? Who tells you about Jesus?

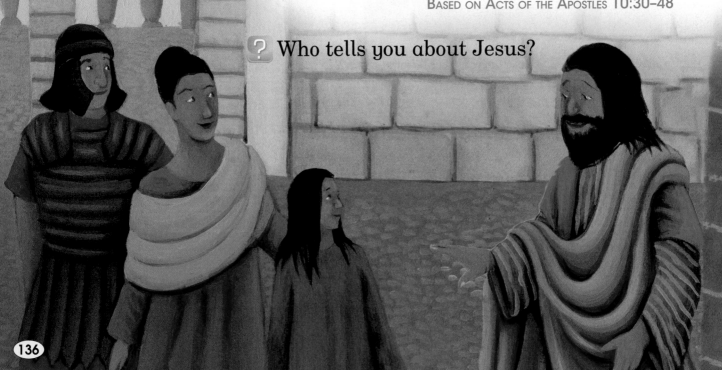

A Prayer of Thanks

Work with a partner to match the numbers to the letters. Finish this prayer.

A	B	C	D	E	F	G	H	I	J	K	L	M
1	2	3	4	5	6	7	8	9	10	11	12	13

N	O	P	Q	R	S	T	U	V	W	X	Y	Z
14	15	16	17	18	19	20	21	22	23	24	25	26

Dear God our Father,

Thank you for your great ___ ___ ___ ___.
12 15 22 5

Thank you for sending us ___ ___ ___ ___ ___.
10   5   19 21 19

Thank you for letting me share in your life through

___ ___ ___ ___ ___ and the Holy Spirit
7   18   1   3   5

in ___ ___ ___ ___ ___ ___ ___.
2   1   16 20   9   19 13

Thank you for welcoming me to your family

and ___ ___ ___ ___ ___ ___. Help me to be a
3   8   21 18   3   8

faithful ___ ___ ___ ___ ___ ___ ___ ___ of Jesus.
6   15 12 12 15 23   5   18

Amen.

Saint Paul the Apostle

As a young man, Paul hated Christians. One day, the Risen Christ appeared to him and changed his life. Paul was baptized and became a friend of Jesus. Paul traveled everywhere to tell everyone about Jesus. He welcomed many people into the Church.

Share In God's Life

We celebrate Baptism with words and
actions. We are dipped into the water or
water is poured over our heads three times.
The priest or deacon prays, "I baptize you
in the name of the Father, and of the Son,
and of the Holy Spirit."

Next, the priest or deacon anoints, or
blesses, the top of our heads with special
oil. We are then dressed in white garments,
and we receive lighted candles.

The words and actions of Baptism show
that we share in God's life. They remind us
that we are followers of Jesus. We are to
live as followers of Jesus, the Light of the
world. We are to be lights in the world
like Jesus.

? What are the four signs or objects used
in the celebration of Baptism?

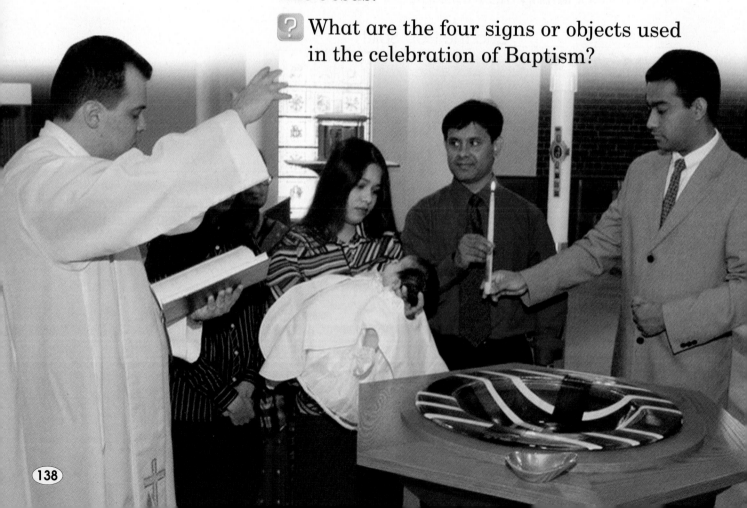

Every time you live your faith in Jesus, you show your love for God. The Holy Spirit helps you to live as a faithful follower of Jesus. He helps you to be a light in the world.

I Follow Jesus

Faithful Ways

Think of how the Holy Spirit helps you live out your Baptism and your faith. On the pathway, write three things you can do to live your faith.

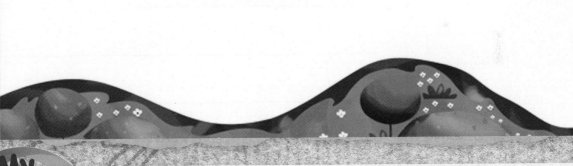

My Faith choice

This week, I will try to live as a faithful follower of Jesus. I will try my best to be a light in the world. I will

_____

_____

_____

 Pray, "Help me, O God, to be a faithful follower of your Son Jesus. Amen."

1. Baptism is the first
Sacrament we
receive.

2. The Sacrament of
Baptism joins us to
Christ and makes
us members of
the Church.

3. The words and
actions of Baptism
show that we
share in God's life.

Chapter Review

Recall

*Find and circle the Sacrament words in the puzzle.
Use the words that you circle in sentences on the
lines below.*

Baptism	**candle**	**white garment**
oil	**water**	**Holy Spirit**

```
H O L Y S P I R I T M C S
W A T E R M D C A N D L E
P W H I T E G A R M E N T
C B A P T I S M Q P O I L
```

_____

_____

_____

_____

_____

Reflect

*Write one way you will live as a follower of Jesus
at school.*

_____

Share Share one way you will live as a
follower of Jesus with your family.

Glory to God

A prayer of adoration gives glory to God.

Leader   Let us give glory to God our Father.

All   **Glory to God, now and forever.**

Leader   Do you believe in God, the Father almighty?

All   **I do.**

Leader   Do you believe in Jesus Christ, his only Son, and our Lord?

All   **I do.**

Leader   Do you believe in the Holy Spirit?

All   **I do.**

Leader   Come forward one at a time. Dip the fingers of your right hand in the bowl of Holy Water. Bless yourself with the Sign of the Cross to remind you of your Baptism.

All   (Dip fingers of your right hand in the Holy Water and make the Sign of the Cross.) **In the name of the Father, and of the Son, and of the Holy Spirit. Amen.**

Give thanks to God!

All   **Glory to God, now and forever. Amen.**

With My Family

This Week . . .

In Chapter 10, "Our Church Welcomes Us," your child learned:

▶ Baptism is the first Sacrament we receive.

▶ Baptism joins us to Christ and makes us members of the Church. We receive the gift of the Holy Spirit. We receive the gift of sanctifying grace. We are made adopted sons and daughters of God.

▶ The Church uses water and oil in the celebration of Baptism.

▶ The virtue of faith is a gift from God that gives us the power to come to know God and believe in him. Living as a faithful follower of Jesus means living out our Baptism.

For more about related teachings of the Church, see the *Catechism of the Catholic Church,* 1213–1284, and the *United States Catholic Catechism for Adults,* pages 183–197.

■ Sharing God's Word

Read together Acts of the Apostles 10:1–49, the account of the Baptism of Cornelius and his family or the version found on page 136. Emphasize that at Baptism, we receive the gift of the Holy Spirit and become adopted sons and daughters of God.

■ Living as Disciples

The Christian home and family is a school of discipleship. Choose one of the following activities to do as a family, or design a similar activity of your own:

▶ After Mass this week, visit the baptismal font in your parish church. Talk about why the Church uses water and other baptismal symbols.

▶ Invite all family members to send thank-you notes to their godparents for all they have done to help them grow up in a life of faith.

■ Our Spiritual Journey

Water is a sign of your Baptism, symbolizing dying to sin, rising to new life, and being made a sharer in the very life of God.

How often each day do you drink water? These times are natural moments to reflect on your dignity as a Christian and your spiritual journey. Invite your children to pray each day, "*Glory to God, now and forever. Amen.*"

For more ideas on ways your family can live as disciples of Jesus, visit **BeMyDisciples.com**

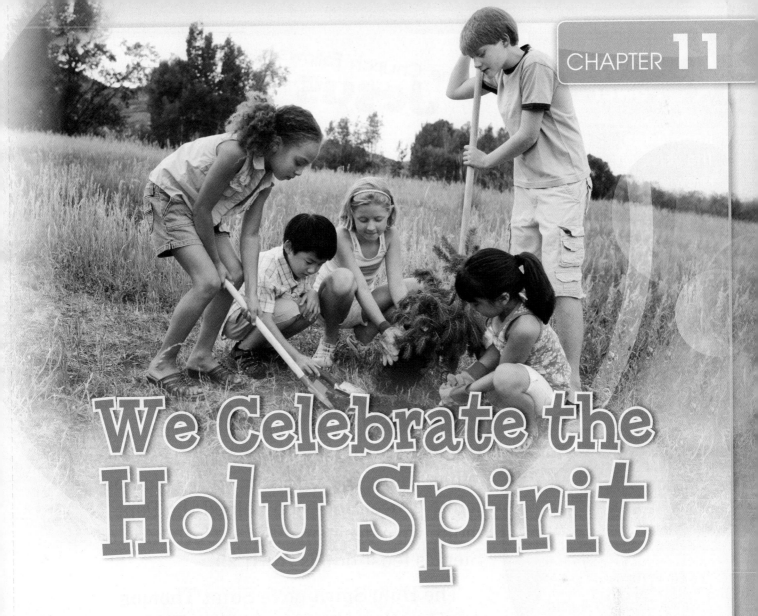

CHAPTER 11

We Celebrate the Holy Spirit

? What special gifts or talents do you have?

Saint Paul reminds us we all have special gifts.

There are different gifts, but one Spirit. The Spirit gives all these gifts so that we can use them to do good things.

BASED ON 1 CORINTHIANS 12:4–11

? How can you use your gifts to help others?

Knowledge
The virtue of knowledge is one of the Gifts of the Holy Spirit. Knowledge helps us better hear and understand the meaning of the Word of God.

The Church Follows **Jesus**

Gifted Saints

The Holy Spirit gives us many gifts to share. The Saints of the Church show us many ways to use those gifts. Saint Catherine of Siena and Saint Thomas Aquinas are two of these Saints.

The Holy Spirit gave Saint Catherine of Siena the gift of wisdom. Catherine used this gift to guide people to live good lives. When there was fighting, she helped people make peace. She even helped the Pope make wise decisions. Saint Catherine of Siena's feast day is April 29.

The Holy Spirit gave Saint Thomas Aquinas the gift of knowledge. Thomas was a great teacher. He wrote many books about the Catholic faith. Thomas helped people learn about their faith. We celebrate his feast on January 28.

❓ How did these two Saints use their gifts?

The gift of wisdom helps us to see how God wants us to live. The gift of knowledge helps us to understand what the Church teaches. You have gifts to share too. These gifts come from God.

? What are the ways that you use your gifts?

Your Gifts

Look at the gifts pictured on this page. In the center of the circle, draw one of the gifts you can share.

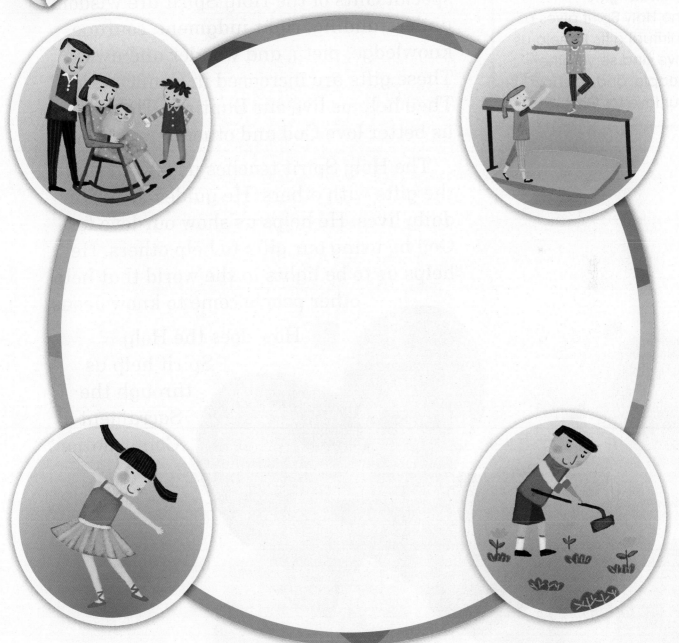

Faith Words
Confirmation
Confirmation is the
Sacrament in which
the gift of the Holy
Spirit strengthens us to
live our Baptism.

spiritual gifts
The Holy Spirit gives us
spiritual gifts to help us
love and serve other
people, and so show
our love for God.

Confirmation

We receive the Sacrament of **Confirmation** after Baptism. In Confirmation, we celebrate and receive the gift of the Holy Spirit.

The Holy Spirit is our teacher, helper, and guide. In Baptism the Holy Spirit gives us seven **spiritual gifts**. These seven special Gifts of the Holy Spirit are wisdom, understanding, right judgment, courage, knowledge, piety, and wonder and awe. These gifts are increased in Confirmation. They help us live our Baptism. They help us better love God and others.

The Holy Spirit teaches us how to share the gifts with others. He guides us in our daily lives. He helps us show our love for God by using our gifts to help others. He helps us to be lights in the world that help other people come to know Jesus.

How does the Holy Spirit help us through the Sacrament of Confirmation?

Activity

The Holy Spirit

Fill in the words that tell you about the Holy Spirit. One has been done for you. Use words from the list below.

SHARE	FAITH	GUIDE	WISDOM
COURAGE	HELPER	TEACHER	PIETY
KNOWLEDGE		SPIRITUAL GIFTS	

H

O

L

Y

S

P

I

S P I R I T U A L   G I F T S

R

I

T

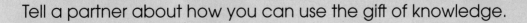

Tell a partner about how you can use the gift of knowledge.

Catholics Believe

Sacred Chrism

Sacred Chrism is special oil that the Church uses in the celebration of some of the Sacraments. It is made from olive oil and balsam. At Confirmation, the bishop marks us with Sacred Chrism in the form of the cross. This is a sign we receive the gift of the Holy Spirit.

Faith Focus
How does the Holy
Spirit help us?

Using Our Spiritual Gifts

You have learned that Paul wrote many letters to the first Christians. In these letters, he reminded them to use the gifts the Holy Spirit gave them. Here is what he wrote to Christians living in Rome:

You are all part of the Body of Christ. The Holy Spirit gives you different gifts. You must use your gifts to share God's love with others.

Show that you love one another. Turn away from what is wrong. Be brave. Do what is right and good. Care for one another. Respect one another. Serve God. Trust in God's promises and be full of hope. Pray and live together in peace.

BASED ON ROMANS 12:5–6, 9–12, 18

[?] How do you use your spiritual gifts?

God wants us to open our hearts to the Holy Spirit. God wants us to use the spiritual gifts the Spirit gives.

? Choose one of the spiritual gifts. What is one way you use this gift?

Activity

Check ✔ **Yes**, if the person is using gifts to share God's love. Check ✔ **No**, if the person is not. Then share how you are using your gifts to share God's love.

	Yes	No
Cameron is a good reader. He does not want to help his little brother learn to read.	☐	☐
Yelina sings well. She sings with the children's choir at Mass.	☐	☐
Diego prays with his sick grandfather.	☐	☐
Ali can draw beautiful pictures. She draws one for Grandma Sue.	☐	☐
Linh is funny, so she makes fun of other children at school.	☐	☐

My gift is _____.

I share this gift by

_____

_____

_____.

Celebrating Confirmation

In Confirmation, the Holy Spirit strengthens us to live our Baptism. The Holy Spirit helps us to remember and share God's love with others.

We celebrate the Sacrament of Confirmation after we are baptized. If we are baptized as infants, we receive this Sacrament when we are older. Grown-ups who are baptized receive Confirmation right after their Baptism.

The bishop usually leads the celebration of Confirmation. During the celebration, he holds hands in the air and prays, "Send your Holy Spirit upon them to be their Helper and Guide." Next, he prays that we will receive Gifts of the Holy Spirit.

Then the bishop places his right hand on top of our heads. He signs our foreheads with Sacred Chrism as he prays, "Be sealed with the Gift of the Holy Spirit." We respond, "Amen."

The bishop then shares a sign of peace with us, saying, "Peace be with you." We answer, "And with your spirit."

? How will you be a follower of Jesus?

God invites you to open your heart to the Holy Spirit. God wants you to use the spiritual gifts you have been given by the Holy Spirit. Three of these gifts are wisdom, courage, and knowledge.

A Gift from the Heart

Activity

Remember that the Holy Spirit has given you spiritual gifts to share. In the heart shape, draw yourself caring for the needs of others.

My Faith Choice

This week, I will use the gift of

_____.

I will

_____.

Pray, "Thank you, Holy Spirit, for your gifts to me. Help me use the gift of courage to use my gifts to help others. Amen."

1. Confirmation is received after the Sacrament of Baptism.

2. In Confirmation, the Holy Spirit gives us spiritual gifts to help us love and serve God and one another.

3. The Sacrament of Confirmation strengthens us to live our Baptism.

Chapter Review

Recall

Circle the word that best completes each sentence.

1. The Church needs the _____ of each person.

   books   **gifts**   **pictures**

2. The Holy Spirit is our _____, helper, and guide.

   priest   **parent**   **teacher**

3. The gift of _____ helps us choose what is good and do what is good.

   courage   **wisdom**   **wonder**

4. In Confirmation, the Church uses _____.

   water   **ashes**   **Sacred Chrism**

5. The _____ usually leads the celebration of Confirmation.

   deacon   **priest**   **bishop**

Reflect

How does using your spiritual gifts help your family?

_____

_____

_____

Share

Write one way the Holy Spirit wants us to use our spiritual gifts with others. Share this with a classmate.

Send Your Spirit

Leader The Holy Spirit teaches us and helps us to pray. God sent the Holy Spirit to help us know that we are God's children. Listen to what the Bible tells us.

Reader *God sent the spirit of his Son into our hearts, crying out, "Abba, Father!"*

Galatians 4:6

The word of the Lord.

All **Thanks be to God.**

Leader Let us pray that we may open our hearts to the Spirit and use the gifts he gives us to help others and to build up the Church. O God, send your Spirit

Group 1 into our hearts that we may love.

All **Holy Spirit be our teacher.**

Leader O God, send your Spirit

Group 2 into our minds that we may understand.

All **Holy Spirit be our helper.**

Leader O God, send your Spirit

Group 3 into our lives that we may serve.

All **Holy Spirit be our teacher.**

Leader Come, Holy Spirit, fill us and guide us. Give us the courage to live as disciples of Jesus. Amen.

With My Family

This Week . . .

In Chapter 11, "We Celebrate the Holy Spirit," your child learned:

▶ We receive the Sacrament of Confirmation after we receive the Sacrament of Baptism.

▶ The Church uses the actions of the laying on of hands and the anointing with Sacred Chrism in the celebration of Confirmation.

▶ In the Sacrament of Confirmation we receive and celebrate the Holy Spirit and his seven spiritual gifts.

▶ The gift of knowledge is one of the seven Gifts of the Holy Spirit. It enables us to discern the meaning of God's Word.

For more about related teachings of the Church, see the *Catechism of the Catholic Church,* 1285–1314 and 1830–1845, and the *United States Catholic Catechism for Adults,* pages 203–209.

■ Sharing God's Word

Read together 1 Corinthians 14:1, 12. Share the gifts your family has to help others and to build up the Church. Talk about how you use them to be lights in the world.

■ Living as Disciples

The Christian home and family is a school of discipleship. Choose one of the following activities to do as a family, or design a similar activity of your own:

▶ After Mass this week visit the place where the sacred oils are kept. Explain that this place is called the ambry. Point out the three containers holding the holy oils; OI stands for Oil of the Sick, OC stands for Oil of Catechumens, and SC stands for Sacred Chrism.

▶ Name some of the times you have seen one another using the gift of knowledge at home. Talk about these, as they are moments you are living your Baptism and are "lights" to one another.

■ Our Spiritual Journey

Almsgiving, or sharing our blessings with others, is one of the three major spiritual disciplines of the Church. While we are used to sharing our material blessings, such as money and food, with those in need, we are also to share our spiritual blessings. Encourage your children to give a portion of any money they receive for the good of others and the Church. This week, pray with your family: *Holy Spirit, be our teacher and helper.*

For more ideas on ways your family can live as disciples of Jesus, visit **BeMyDisciples.com**

CHAPTER 12

We Celebrate Forgiveness

? What do you say when you need forgiveness?

Listen carefully to what happens in Heaven when someone asks forgiveness for doing wrong.

There is great joy in heaven for one who asks for forgiveness. BASED ON LUKE 15:7

? Why do you think this causes great joy in Heaven?

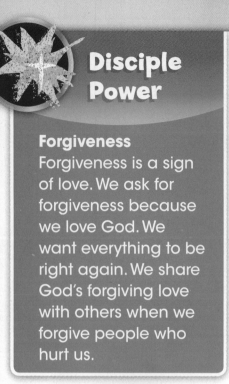

Forgiveness
Forgiveness is a sign of love. We ask for forgiveness because we love God. We want everything to be right again. We share God's forgiving love with others when we forgive people who hurt us.

Saint John Vianney

Jesus taught his followers about forgiveness. He taught them that they are to forgive over and over again.

Saint John Vianney was a priest. He was honored and respected because of his kindness to people who were sorry for their sins. Through forgiveness, he showed people God's mercy and love. Saint John Vianney was a special sign of God's forgiveness.

There is a story that a special railroad track was built to the village where Father John Vianney lived. The railroad track was built because so many people from all over France wanted to come to John Vianney to confess their sins.

John Vianney was named a Saint in 1925. He is the patron Saint of parish priests.

? How was Saint John Vianney a sign of God's forgiving love?

Sometimes we need to forgive others. And sometimes we need to ask others to forgive us.

? How can we be a sign of God's forgiving love?

Forgiving Ways

Read the short stories. Decide what each person might say or do.

Shawna's dad gave her a special balloon for her birthday. Malik teases her and pops the balloon.

- To make things okay again, what can Malik say or do?

- What can Shawna say or do?

Randy is on the computer doing homework. His older sister Becca sends him a hurtful message that makes fun of him.

- To make things right again, what might Randy say or do?

- What might Becca say or do?

FORGIVENESS

Faith Words

sin
Sin is to freely choose
to do or say something
we know God does not
want us to do or to say.

Penance and Reconciliation

Each day we make many choices. Most of the time, we make good choices. Sometimes we choose to do or say something that we know God does not want us to do or say. This is called a **sin**.

Sometimes we may choose not to do or say something we know God wants us to do or say. This also is a sin. Sin always harms our friendship with God and with other people.

When we sin, we need to turn to God and other people and ask for forgiveness. We also need to make things better when we sin.

The Holy Spirit helps us to ask for forgiveness. We need to say, "I am sorry. Please forgive me." This shows we are truly sorry for our sins. God hears and forgives us when we say we are sorry for our sins.

❓ What do we need to do when we sin?

Heartfelt Forgiveness

Look at the heart. On the side marked *FORGIVE,* write or draw about someone you need to forgive. On the side marked *ASK FORGIVENESS,* write or draw about someone you need to ask for forgiveness.

Act of Contrition

When we celebrate the Sacrament of Penance and Reconciliation, we may pray an act of contrition. In this prayer, we tell God we are sorry for our sins, ask for forgiveness, and tell God we will try our best not to sin again.

ASK FORGIVENESS

FORGIVE

Practice signing, "I'm sorry."

I'm

sorry.

The Forgiving Father

Jesus told a story about forgiveness.

A father had two sons. The younger son told his father, "I want my share of the family's money now." The father gave the son his share of the family money. The son left home and quickly wasted his money.

The son thought about his home and his father. He was very sorry for what he had done and decided to return home.

The father saw his son walking toward the family home. The father ran down the road to welcome his son back home. The father hugged his son and kissed him. The son said, "Father, I am very sorry." The father was so happy that he gave a big party to celebrate.

BASED ON LUKE 15:11–24

? **What do you think Jesus was teaching about God in this story?**

Jesus wants us to know that God loves and forgives us. When we are sorry and ask God for forgiveness for our sins, God forgives us. God rejoices and welcomes us back home.

? What are ways you can show forgiveness?

Activity

God's Forgiveness

Find your way to God's forgiveness. Draw a line to find your way to forgiveness.

I did something wrong.

I'm sorry.

I promise to do better.

I want to come back home to God.

I ask for forgiveness.

You are forgiven. Let's celebrate!

Faith Words

reconciliation
Reconciliation means to become friends again.

penance
Penance is something we do or say to show we are truly sorry for the choices we made to hurt someone.

We Celebrate Reconciliation

We too need to ask for forgiveness when we sin. Jesus gave us a Sacrament to help us do this. It is called the Sacrament of **Penance** and **Reconciliation**.

In this Sacrament, we share in God's mercy and forgiving love. God is always ready to forgive us if we are sorry for our sins. Our sins are forgiven. We receive God's grace. God's grace helps us to make good choices to live as children of God. We receive the gift of peace.

Every celebration of this Sacrament always has four parts. The four parts are:

1. **Confession.** We meet with the priest by ourselves and tell him our sins.

2. **Contrition.** We tell God we are truly sorry for our sins. We pray an act of contrition.

3. **Penance.** We are given a penance. Doing our penance helps repair, or heal, the harm we have caused by our sins.

4. **Absolution.** The priest lays his hands on or over our heads while he says a special prayer. The words and actions of the priest tell us we have received God's forgiveness.

How does the Sacrament of Penance and Reconciliation help us?

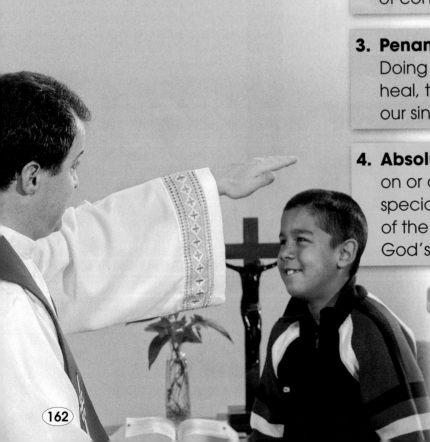

In the Sacrament of Penance and Reconciliation, God forgives you. You need to forgive others as God forgives you. When you forgive others, you are acting with kindness. You are a peacemaker.

I Follow Jesus

Activity

Sharing God's Gift of Forgiveness

Fill in the empty spaces. Describe how you can be a peacemaker.

I can ask the Holy Spirit to help me live as a peacemaker.

I will forgive _____.

I will show my forgiveness by saying _____.

I will show my forgiveness by doing _____.

My Faith Choice

This week, I will forgive others. I will do what I have written on the lines above.

Pray, "Thank you, Father, for your mercy and kindness. Holy Spirit, teach and help me to be forgiving as Jesus taught. Amen."

1. Sin is choosing to do or say something against God.

2. In the Sacrament of Penance and Reconciliation, we ask for and receive forgiveness for our sins.

3. Contrition, confession, penance, and absolution are always part of the Sacrament of Penance and Reconciliation.

Chapter Review

Recall

Complete the sentences. Use the words in the word bank.

Absolution	Confession
Contrition	Penance

1. _____ is the telling of our sins to the priest.

2. _____ is true sorrow for our sins.

3. _____ is making up for our sins.

4. _____ is receiving God's forgiveness for our sins.

Reflect

Why is forgiveness important in your life to be a follower of Jesus?

_____

_____

_____

_____

_____.

Share Write and then share with a classmate how you have forgiven someone.

Prayer of Petition

In a prayer of petition, we believe and trust that God will hear our prayers and help us.

Leader   God is always ready to forgive us and to welcome us home. Let us listen to the Word of God.

Reader   A reading from the holy Gospel according to John.

All   **Glory to you, O Lord.**

Reader   *John 20:19–23.*
The Gospel of the Lord.

All   **Praise to you, Lord Jesus Christ.**

Leader   Lord, our God, you always forgive us because of your great love.

All   **Fill our hearts with joy.**

Leader   For the times we did what was wrong, we pray,

All   **Forgive us and welcome us home.**

Leader   For the times we did not forgive others, we pray,

All   **Forgive us and welcome us home.**

Leader   Lord, our God, you always forgive us.

All   **Fill our hearts with peace.
Amen.**

With My Family

This Week . . .

In Chapter 12, "We Celebrate Forgiveness," your child learned:

▶ Jesus gave the Church the Sacrament of Penance and Reconciliation.

▶ Sin harms our relationship with God and others. When we sin, we need to seek forgiveness.

▶ In the Sacrament of Penance and Reconciliation, we ask for and receive God's forgiveness for the sins we have committed after Baptism. This Sacrament reconciles us with God and with the Church.

▶ When we practice the virtue of forgiveness we offer God's forgiving love to others.

For more about related teachings of the Church, see the *Catechism of the Catholic Church,* 545–546, 587–590, 976–983, 1846–1848, and 1420–1484, and the *United States Catholic Catechism for Adults,* pages 234–243.

■ Sharing God's Word

Read together Luke 15:11–24, the parable of the Forgiving Father (Prodigal Son). Or read the adaptation of the parable on page 160. Emphasize the joy of the forgiving father when his prodigal son returned home. Talk about the joy and peace the members of your family experience when you forgive one another.

■ Living as Disciples

The Christian home and family is a school of discipleship. Choose one of the following activities to do as a family, or design a similar activity of your own:

▶ Discuss ways your family members ask for forgiveness and forgive one another. Discuss why it is important to forgive one another. Emphasize that when we forgive someone it does not mean that what the person did to hurt us is all right.

▶ Ask each family member to name some of the ways they have been a peacemaker at home. Promise to help one another live as a family of peacemakers. At dinnertime this week, pray to the Holy Spirit to help you live as peacemakers.

■ Our Spiritual Journey

At the heart of Jesus' work is forgiveness and reconciliation. The Hebrew word *mercy* cannot be easily translated into English. It points to the infinite mercy of God and the undeserved and limitless nature of divine forgiveness. This is the forgiveness we are to show others. Pray the Prayer of Petition for forgiveness with your family this week.

For more ideas on ways your family can live as disciples of Jesus, visit **BeMyDisciples.com**

Kids for Peace

Kids for Peace is a world-wide group made up of kids who want to be peacemakers. Young persons who are part of Kids for Peace work to serve others. They act with kindness. They respect others. They care for the Earth, and they believe that they are neighbors with people all over the world.

Members of Kids for Peace make a peace pledge. A pledge is a special promise. This is the promise they make:

WE MAKE PEACE

Everyone who wants peace must work for justice. When we care for others, act with kindness, and respect all people, we are being peacemakers.

heiwa Pokój salam

Paix Pax

I pledge to use my words
  to speak in a kind way.

I pledge to help others
  as I go throughout my day.

I pledge to care for our earth
  with my healing heart and hands.

I pledge to respect people
  in each and every land.

I pledge to join together
  as we unite the big and small.

I pledge to do my part
  to create PEACE for one and all.

Achukma Peace shalom

paz Hòa Bình

Making Connections

Peace is Jesus' promise, gift, and command. Jesus calls us to make peace, and he calls peacemakers, "children of God" (Matthew 5:9). When we work for peace, we are acting as God's own children.

with Creative Arts

Make a handprint peace wreath. Everyone trace their hands, color them, cut them out, and then, on tag board, paste them together to form a wreath. Make a dove shape for the center of the wreath. Post the wreath in the classroom.

with Language Arts

Make a list of the Disciple Power words you have discovered. Each one is a virtue or gift that can help you act as a peacemaker. Choose two of the Disciple Power words. Write each one on an index card. Then write how the two virtues you chose will help you be a peacemaker. Choose to do what you write.

with Social Studies

Look at the words found on page 167. Each word is in a different language, but each means, *Peace*. Find the country of the language you chose on a map. Write a prayer for peace and use the peace word in the language you chose. Pray for peace in that country and in the world.

Faith Action

Decide on one way you can be a peacemaker in your family or at your school. One way I will choose to be a peacemaker is _____

_____

_____.

Unit 3 Review

A. Choose the Best Word

Complete the sentences. Color the circle next to the best choice for each sentence.

1. The Seven _____ are signs of God's love for us.

○ Bibles   ○ Sacraments   ○ Prayers

2. Water and oil are used in the Sacrament of _____.

○ Baptism   ○ Penance and Reconciliation

○ Matrimony

3. Jesus told the story of the Forgiving _____ to teach us about God's forgiveness.

○ Son   ○ Brother   ○ Father

4. In the Sacrament of Confirmation, we receive _____.

○ Jesus   ○ spiritual gifts   ○ forgiveness

5. _____ is freely choosing to do or say something we know God does not want us to do or to say.

○ Penance   ○ Reconciliation   ○ Sin

B. Show What You Know

Draw a line to connect the clues to the correct Sacrament.

Sacrament

1. Baptism

2. Confirmation

3. Penance and Reconciliation

Clue

a. strengthens us by the Holy Spirit

b. forgiveness of sins committed after Baptism

c. first Sacrament we receive

C. Connect with Scripture

What was your favorite story about Jesus in this unit?
Draw something that happened in the story.
Tell your class about it.

D. Be a Disciple

1. *What Saint or holy person did you enjoy hearing about in this unit? Write the name here. Tell your class what this person did to follow Jesus.*

_____

_____

2. *What can you do to be a good disciple of Jesus?*

_____

_____

"Thank You, Jesus"

One day, Jesus met ten sick people by the side of the road. They had an awful sickness called leprosy.

When the ten saw Jesus, they called out to him. "Jesus, help us!" they shouted. "Jesus, have mercy on us!" they cried.

Jesus healed all ten people. As they were leaving, one of the ten turned right around to thank Jesus. "Praise God!" he shouted. "Thank you, Jesus!"

Jesus smiled and said, "Stand up and go; your faith has saved you."

BASED ON LUKE 17:11–19

What I Know

What is something you already know about these faith concepts?

The Liturgy of the Word

_____

_____

The Liturgy of the Eucharist

_____

_____

Mission

_____

_____

Put an X next to the faith words you know. Put a ? next to the faith words you need to learn more about.

_____ Mass   _____ Gospel   _____ Eucharist
                 Acclamation
_____ assembly   _____ procession

What do you know about God's promises to his people in the Bible?

_____

A Question I Have

What question would you like to ask about the Mass?

_____

_____

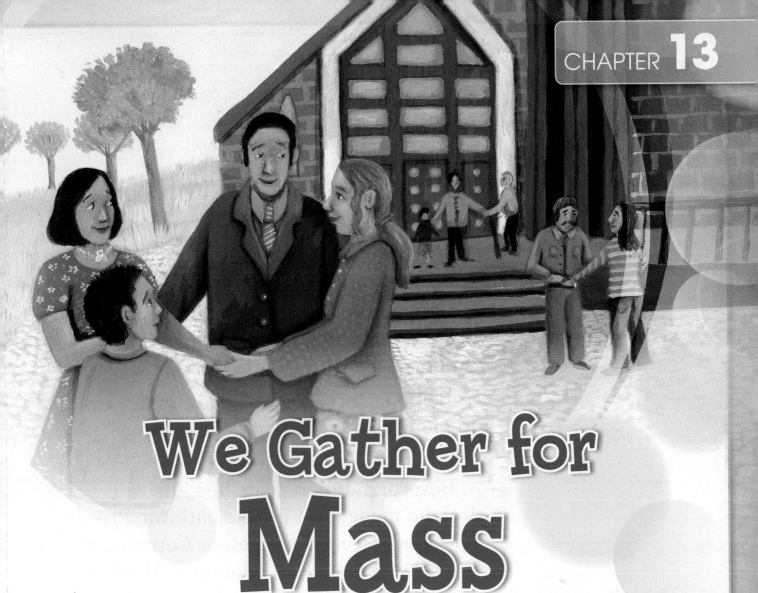

CHAPTER 13

We Gather for Mass

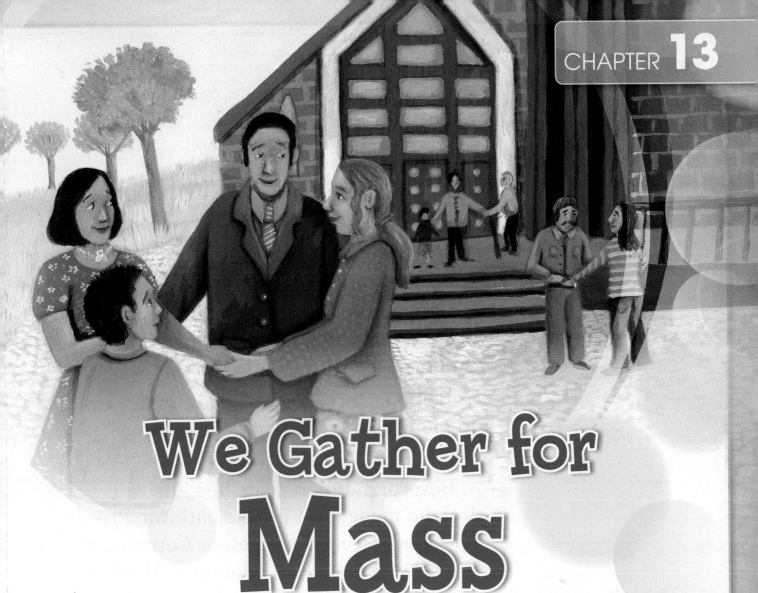 When do families gather to celebrate?

God invites us to gather to celebrate. Listen to what God says to his people.

Call my people together. Gather all the people. Gather the old, the young, even the babies. Rejoice and celebrate. Worship the Lord, your God! BASED ON JOEL 2:15–16, 23

 When do Catholics gather to worship God?

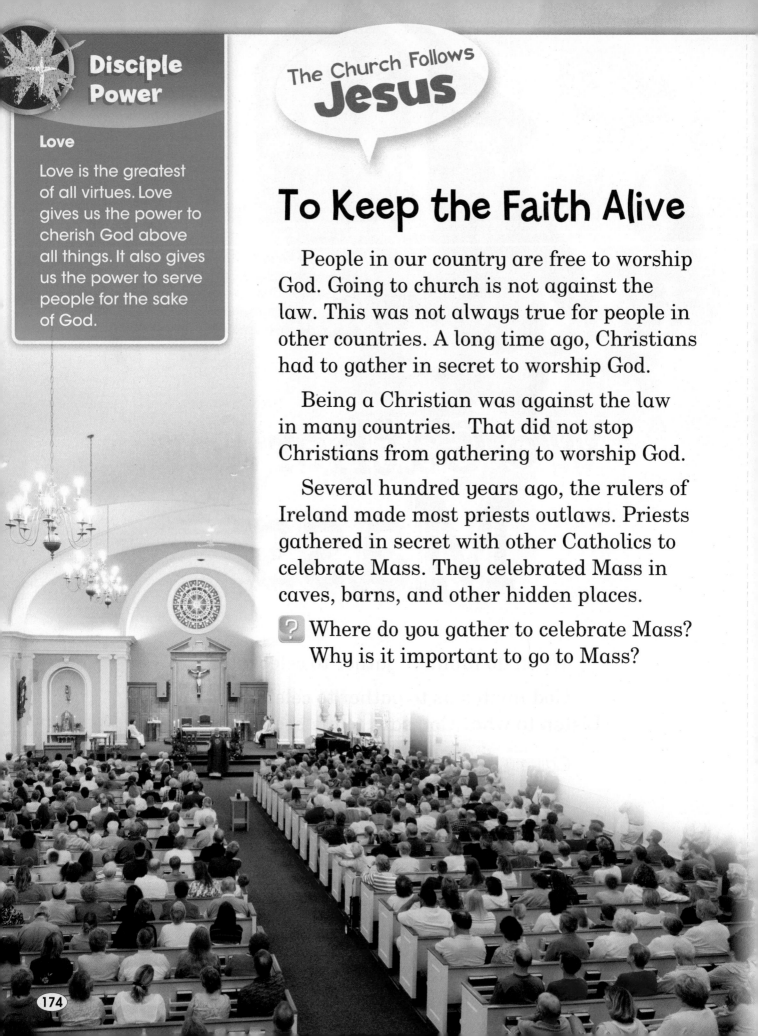

Love

Love is the greatest of all virtues. Love gives us the power to cherish God above all things. It also gives us the power to serve people for the sake of God.

The Church Follows
Jesus

To Keep the Faith Alive

People in our country are free to worship God. Going to church is not against the law. This was not always true for people in other countries. A long time ago, Christians had to gather in secret to worship God.

Being a Christian was against the law in many countries. That did not stop Christians from gathering to worship God.

Several hundred years ago, the rulers of Ireland made most priests outlaws. Priests gathered in secret with other Catholics to celebrate Mass. They celebrated Mass in caves, barns, and other hidden places.

? Where do you gather to celebrate Mass? Why is it important to go to Mass?

Not long ago, the government of the Czech Republic did not want people to be Catholic. But Father Petr Pit'ha and many other priests continued to gather people for Mass and other Sacraments. Today, Catholics in that country can celebrate their faith without fear.

? **What are ways that we celebrate our faith?**

Giving Praise to God

Complete this prayer.

Loving God,

Thank you for calling me to worship and celebrate your love.

Thank you for my parish church,

_____

where I can gather with others for prayer and praise.

Thank you for the people with whom I gather, especially for

_____

_____

_____

Thank you for my parish priest, Father _____,
who leads us in celebration.

Thank you most of all for your Son, Jesus, who is with us whenever we gather in his name. Amen.

Faith Words

Mass
The Mass is the most important celebration of the Church. At Mass, we gather to worship God. We listen to God's Word. We celebrate and share in the Eucharist.

assembly
The assembly is the People of God gathered to celebrate Mass. All members of the assembly share in the celebration of Mass.

We Gather at Mass

Jesus gathered people. He invited people to come together on mountainsides, near lakes, and around tables in homes. He gathered people to share the good news of God's love. Jesus promised,

For where two or three are gathered together in my name, there am I in the midst of them.

MATTHEW 18:20

After Jesus rose from the dead and returned to God, his followers came together. They gathered to pray and listen to God's Word. They remembered Jesus and shared in the Eucharist.

The followers gathered to listen to the teaching of the Apostles, to break bread, and to pray together.

BASED ON ACTS OF THE APOSTLES 2:42

? What do you do when you gather together with your Church family at Mass?

Today we gather too. Every Sunday, we come together to worship God in the celebration of the **Mass**.

At Mass, Catholics gather as an **assembly**. We come to Mass. We pray aloud and sing. We stand and sit and kneel. We show we are disciples of Jesus. Together we worship God the Holy Trinity.

? Why do we gather as an assembly at Mass?

Activity

With a partner, talk about all of the things you do at Mass. Choose one thing and draw it in the space. Then together, act it out for the class.

Faith Focus
What happens when
we gather for Mass?

The Mass Begins

The Mass is the most important celebration of the Church. We gather together in church with our Catholic community. We take our place as part of the assembly.

When we gather for Mass, we show that we are disciples of Jesus. We gather to praise God the Father for the great gift of Jesus. We give thanks to God for all our blessings.

The Entrance

The Introductory Rites begin the celebration of Mass. The priest or bishop and other ministers enter in procession. Only a priest or bishop can lead us in the celebration of Mass. He wears special clothes called vestments.

We stand and sing. The cantor, or song leader, leads us in the entrance hymn. Singing helps to join us together. We sing our praise and thanks to God.

How does gathering for Mass show that we are disciples of Jesus?

Sign of the Cross and the Greeting

The priest welcomes or greets us. He leads the assembly in praying the Sign of the Cross. This reminds us how Jesus gave himself for us on the Cross. We also remember our Baptism.

Then the priest greets us with open arms, saying, "The Lord be with you." We respond, "And with your spirit." These words remind us that God is with us in our gathering.

? How does the celebration of the Mass begin?

Gathering at Mass

Write the names of those who helped you participate in Mass last Sunday.

• With whom did you assemble?

_____

• Who led the assembly in song?

_____

• Who led the assembly in prayer?

_____

Faith Focus
What are the
other parts of the
Introductory Rites of
the Mass?

The Assembly Prays

The Introductory Rites of the Mass continue after the Sign of the Cross and the greeting. Together we pray special prayers.

Penitential Act

After the greeting, the priest invites us to remember God's forgiving love. We pray aloud, asking for the Lord's mercy.

The Gloria

On most Sundays, we sing or pray aloud a special hymn called the "Gloria." It is a beautiful hymn of thanks and praise. This is how it begins.

Glory to God in the highest,
and on earth peace to people of good will.

The Collect

The priest then says, "Let us pray." We spend a moment in silent prayer. Then the priest leads us in the Collect. This prayer collects all our prayers and brings them to God the Father in the name of Jesus. We respond to the prayer by saying, "Amen."

? What do we do in the Introductory Rites of the Mass?

A song leader at Mass

On Sunday, you and your family gather with your Church family to worship God. You offer God thanks and praise together.

 Draw yourself gathered with your Church family for worship. In your picture, show how you are worshiping God at Mass.

The Church Family Gathers

 I will pay attention at Mass. I will help my family take part in Mass on Sunday. I will

_____

_____

 Pray, "Gather me in your love, O God, so I can offer you praise. Amen."

Chapter Review

Recall

Number the sentences in the order in which these actions happen at Mass.

_____ **A.** The priest greets us, and we pray the Sign of the Cross.

_____ **B.** We sing or pray aloud the "Gloria."

_____ **C.** The priest leads us in the Collect.

_____ **D.** We pray for the Lord's mercy.

_____ **E.** The priest enters in procession.

Reflect

In what ways do you prepare to worship God?

_____

_____

_____

_____

_____

Share   Share with a classmate your favorite part of the Mass and why.

Praise God

At Mass, we offer God thanks and praise. We pray aloud or sing with joy. Pray this psalm of joy with your class.

Leader

Loving God, we gather in your name to give you thanks and praise.

Group 1

Shout with joy to God, all the Earth.
Worship the Lord with gladness.
Come before him singing for joy.

All

Shout with joy to God, all the Earth.

Group 2

Enter God's gates with thanksgiving.
Go into God's presence with praise.
Indeed, let us give thanks and bless God's name.

All

Shout with joy to God, all the Earth.

Group 3

The Lord our God is good;
He is kind and merciful.
His faithful love lasts forever.

All

Shout with joy to God, all the Earth.

BASED ON PSALM 100

With My Family

This Week . . .

In Chapter 13, "We Gather for Mass," your child learned:

▶ The Mass is the Church's most important celebration.

▶ At Mass, we gather as an assembly—the Church, the People of God. Together we take part in the Eucharistic celebration.

▶ The celebration of Mass begins with the Introductory Rites. We prepare ourselves for the celebration of God's Word and of the Eucharist.

▶ The virtue of love empowers us to love God and love others because of our love for God.

For more about related teachings of the Church, see the *Catechism of the Catholic Church*, 1322–1332 and 1346 and 1348, and the *United States Catholic Catechism for Adults*, pages 215–227.

■ Sharing God's Word

Read together Acts of the Apostles 2:42–47, an account of the gathering of the early Church. Emphasize that from the beginning of the Church, Christians gathered to listen to the teachings and writings of the Apostles and to celebrate the Eucharist.

■ Living as Disciples

The Christian home and family is a school of discipleship. Choose one of the following activities to do as a family, or design a similar activity of your own.

▶ Form the habit of reading the upcoming Sunday readings before Mass. You can find them at the *Be My Disciples* Web site, or in special books for this purpose. On the way home, discuss the readings and the homily.

▶ Talk about the different ways your family gets ready to gather for Mass. Point out that these activities are all part of preparing to celebrate the Eucharist. These moments, too, can be a form of prayer.

■ Our Spiritual Journey

The Theological Virtues of faith, hope, and love invite and empower us to glorify God in all we say and do. Deepen your understanding of these virtues. They are the driving power that enables you to respond and give direction to your response, "Here I am, Lord. Send me." Teach this prayer to your child.

For more ideas on ways your family can live as disciples of Jesus, visit **BeMyDisciples.com**

CHAPTER 14

We Listen to God's Word

? What stories or words do you like to hear over and over?

Here is a story we hear at Mass. Jesus was helping people in a village. He was teaching them about God's love. Then something surprising happened.

> A woman said in a loud voice, "Blessed is your mother to have such a wonderful son." Jesus said to the woman, "Blessed are those who hear the Word of God and keep it."   Based on Luke 11:27–28

? What does it mean to keep the Word of God?

Compassion

Compassion means to care about others when they are hurt or feeling sad. Having compassion makes us want to help them feel better.

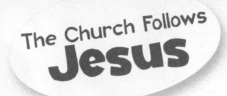

The Church Follows **Jesus**

Announcing God's Word

Jesus told us that he is the Word of God. When we listen to Jesus and do what he says, we are blessed. We are friends of God.

Jesus had Good News from his Father to share with everyone. But what if you could not hear God's Word?

The Catholic Church helps everyone come to know Jesus. They show compassion to all who need help. Pope Benedict XVI said that deaf people are not only hearers of the Word of God, but also "its announcers."

Deaf people can learn to hear and share God's Word. They use a language of hand gestures called American Sign Language, or ASL.

Many priests, deacons, brothers, sisters, and laypeople work with people who cannot hear at all and with people who are hard-of-hearing. They teach the Catholic faith. They share the Word of God using ASL.

? How can people who are deaf and hard-of-hearing be hearers and announcers of God's Word?

In many parishes, someone signs the words that the priest and others say aloud at Mass. The deaf and hard-of-hearing people sign their responses.

Activity

Signing the Word of God

What do you think the person in the pictures below is saying in ASL? Hint: It is the Word of God from Luke 11:28. Write the words on the lines.

_____

_____

_____

_____

_____

_____

Faith Words
Liturgy of the Word
The Liturgy of the Word is the first main part of the Mass. God speaks to us through the readings from the Bible.

The Liturgy of the Word

After the Introductory Rites, we celebrate the **Liturgy of the Word.** The Liturgy of the Word is the first main part of the Mass. We listen and respond to God's Word.

The Readings from the Bible

At Mass on Sundays and on Saturday evenings, we listen to three readings. We sit for the first two readings.

The First Reading is usually from the Old Testament. We hear stories about God's people who lived many years before Jesus.

After the first reading, we sing or pray the Responsorial Psalm. Then we listen to the Second Reading. It is from the New Testament. We hear stories about the first Christian communities.

At the end of both the first and the second readings, the reader says, "The word of the Lord." We respond, "Thanks be to God."

? Why do you think we say, "Thanks be to God" after we listen to the readings?

A reading from one of the four Gospels comes next. We get ready to listen to the Gospel by standing and singing or praying aloud the Gospel Acclamation. This is a short hymn of praise. On most days, we stand and sing, "Alleluia." This word means "Praise the Lord!"

 Why do you think we sing or say "Alleluia," before we listen to the Gospel?

Catholics Believe

The Sanctuary

The sanctuary is the place in the church where you see the altar and the ambo. The word sanctuary means "holy place." The ambo is the stand where the readers, the deacon, and the priest proclaim the Word of God.

Activity

Praying Alleluia

Learn to sign this word that we say or sing at Mass.

Alleluia!

Write the meaning of the word, Alleluia, below.

_____

_____

Faith Focus
Why do we stand
when the Gospel is
proclaimed?

We Listen to God's Word

The deacon or priest proclaims the Gospel. The Gospel is the Good News of Jesus Christ. We stand to show our respect.

Listen to this Gospel reading about the Kingdom of God. Jesus said,

"What is the kingdom of God like? It is like a tiny mustard seed. A person takes the mustard seed and plants it in the garden. The tiny seed grows and when it becomes fully grown, it becomes a large tree. Birds in the sky build nests in the branches of the tree."

BASED ON LUKE 13:18–19

The Kingdom of God will grow with all the people who will love God. This is the Good News of Jesus Christ.

? How is a tiny mustard seed like the Kingdom of God?

When the priest or deacon finishes the reading, he holds up the Book of the Gospels for all to see and says, "The Gospel of the Lord." The assembly responds, "Praise to you, Lord Jesus Christ." With these words, we thank Jesus for showing us God's love.

❓ Why is the Gospel reading important?

Activity

Learn to sign the response to the Gospel reading at Mass.

Praise

you

Lord

Jesus

Christ

"Praise to you, Lord Jesus Christ."

Faith Focus
What happens during
the Liturgy of the Word
after the Gospel?

We Respond to God's Word

The Homily

After the Gospel is proclaimed, we sit. The priest or deacon talks to us. He helps us to understand the readings. This is called the Homily.

The Profession of Faith

After the Homily, we stand. Together we respond to God's Word. We pray aloud a profession of faith, or a creed of the Church. We say we believe in God the Father, God the Son, and God the Holy Spirit.

The Prayer of the Faithful

The last part of the Liturgy of the Word is the Prayer of the Faithful. We ask God to help the Church and our country. We pray for other people and for ourselves. We ask God's help for everyone.

? How do we respond to the Word of God?

At Mass, you are part of the assembly. You take part in the celebration of Mass in many ways. During the Liturgy of the Word, you listen and respond to the Word of God.

I Follow Jesus

Activity

I Listen and Respond

Draw or write about a Bible story you heard at Mass. Write the title of your story on the line. Share what the story tells you about God's love.

_____

My Faith Choice

The next time I take part in Mass, I will

☐ say the responses   ☐ sing the hymns

☐ listen carefully   ☐ pray the profession
   to the readings   of faith

☐ _____."

Pray, "Open my ears to hear your Word, O God. Open my heart to live it every day. Amen."

1. The Liturgy of the
   Word is the first
   main part of the
   Mass.

2. The Gospel is
   the main part of
   the Liturgy of the
   Word.

3. At Mass, we listen
   and respond to
   the Word of God.

Chapter Review

Recall

Match each word with its correct description.

Words	Descriptions
_____ 1. readings	**a.** The priest or deacon helps us to understand God's Word.
_____ 2. Homily	**b.** We profess our faith in God the Father, God the Son, and God the Holy Spirit.
_____ 3. creed	**c.** We listen to God's Word.
_____ 4. Prayer of the Faithful	**d.** We ask God to help us and other people.

Number the parts of the Liturgy of the Word in the correct order that they happen during Mass.

_____ Profession of Faith   _____ Responsorial Psalm

_____ Prayer of the Faithful   _____ New Testament Reading

_____ Homily   _____ Old Testament Reading

                                    _____ Gospel

Reflect

What is one way the Liturgy of the Word can help you?

_____

_____

Share After Mass this week, share what you learned from the Homily with your family.

Lord, Hear Our Prayer

At Mass we sometimes pray "Lord, hear our prayer" during the Prayer of the Faithful. This shows that we believe God is with us.

All   **(Pray the Sign of the Cross.)**

Leader   Let us pray.
God our Father, we ask for your help. We pray for the Church, for our country, for our family, and for our friends. We pray for people who are sick. We pray for all people.

All   **Lord, hear our prayer.**

Leader   We pray for people who are sick.

All   **Lord, hear our prayer.**

Student   For _____, we pray to the Lord.

All   **Lord, hear our prayer.**

Leader   God our Father, send the Holy Spirit upon all who need your help.
We ask this in the name of Jesus.

All   **Amen.**

With My Family

This Week . . .

In Chapter 14, "We Listen to God's Word," your child learned:

▶ The Liturgy of the Word is the first main part of the Mass.

▶ The Gospel is the center of the Liturgy of the Word.

▶ During the Liturgy of the Word, we listen to God's Word and make it part of our lives.

▶ We profess our faith and pray for the living and the dead.

▶ The quality of compassion helps us to respond to the needs of others.

For more about related teachings of the Church, see the *Catechism of the Catholic Church*, 1322–1332, and 1346 and 1349, and the *United States Catholic Catechism for Adults*, page 218.

■ Sharing God's Word

Read together 1 Timothy 3:16. Discuss how Scripture can help your family find ways to offer compassion to others like Jesus. Talk about ways you can make reading the Scripture something you do each day.

■ Living as Disciples

The Christian home and family is a school of discipleship. Choose one of the following activities to do as a family, or design a similar activity of your own.

▶ Read to your child every day—stories, the Bible, even the daily paper. Listening to a reading is not only pleasing but helps prepare us to listen to the proclamation of God's Word in the liturgy.

▶ Review the responses for the Liturgy of the Word with your child. These can be found on pages 188–191 in your child's book. Knowing the responses helps us better participate in the Mass.

■ Our Spiritual Journey

At Mass, the Prayer of the Faithful allows us to pray to God for the needs of others. Helping your child to form the habit of praying for the needs of others helps him or her to see the world through a wder perspective and to remember that God brings all blessings. Pray the prayer on page 195 together at home.

For more ideas on ways your family can live as disciples of Jesus, visit **BeMyDisciples.com**

CHAPTER 15

We Give Thanks

? What is a gift you have received?

All good things come from God. Think of your many blessings. Join with all God's people and pray,

I will join with your people, Lord God.
I will thank you in the great assembly.

BASED ON PSALM 35:18

? What do you want to thank God for?

Thankfulness

Thankfulness is a big part of who we are as disciples of Jesus. We have received wonderful blessings and gifts. Jesus calls us to be a thankful people.

The Church Follows Jesus

Thank You, Lord

Saint Francis of Assisi knew all his blessings came from God. Francis was so full of joy, he often sang his thanks to God.

Catholics thank God for their blessings in many ways. Today the followers of Saint Francis are called Franciscans. The Franciscans in New York City say thanks to God every day. One way they do this is by sharing their blessings with people.

People in New York City who need food or clothing come to the Church of Saint Francis of Assisi. The Franciscans are there every morning to greet them.

The Franciscans give each person sandwiches and something to drink and sometimes clothing to wear. Most importantly, the Franciscans share a smile and words of welcome. Franciscans continue to share love and respect just as Jesus and Saint Francis did.

? What ways can you and your family give thanks to God by sharing with others?

Listen to what God's people said in the Bible.

Give thanks to the LORD, for he is good,
for his kindness endures forever.

1 CHRONICLES 16:34

Just like God's people and Saint Francis, we give thanks and praise to God today.

? What is one way you praise God?

Activity

Giving Thanks

Write four things for which you are especially thankful.

_____   _____

_____   _____

Draw a picture that shows how you can show your thankfulness by sharing love and respect just as Jesus did.

Faith Words

Liturgy of the Eucharist
The Liturgy of the Eucharist is the second main part of the Mass. The Church does what Jesus did at the Last Supper.

Eucharist
The Eucharist is the Sacrament of the Body and Blood of Jesus Christ.

The Liturgy of the Eucharist

The Church celebrates the **Liturgy of the Eucharist** as the second main part of the Mass. The word *eucharist* means "thanksgiving."

The **Eucharist** is the Sacrament of the Body and Blood of Jesus Christ. During the Liturgy of the Eucharist at Mass, we give thanks to God for all he has done for us. At Mass, we give thanks to God for the gift of Jesus.

The Preparation of the Gifts

The Liturgy of the Eucharist begins with the Preparation of the Gifts. Members of the assembly bring the gifts of bread and wine to the altar.

This procession is important. It shows that we are bringing our love for God and others to the altar with the bread and wine.

? What are the ways the Church gives thanks at Mass?

The priest accepts our gifts and places them on the altar. Then he tells God all our blessings come from him. We respond, "Blessed be God for ever." We call these blessing prayers. When we pray a blessing prayer, we are telling God that he is the maker of everything good.

After he washes his hands, the priest invites us to pray. He then leads us in the Prayer Over the Offerings. We respond, "Amen."

? What are the ways you and your family give thanks to God?

Catholics Believe

The Holy Sacrifice

The Mass is also called the Holy Sacrifice. Jesus' sacrifice on the Cross is the greatest act of love for God the Father and for all people. At Mass, we are made sharers in the sacrifice of Jesus. We join with Jesus and show our love for God. We receive God's grace to love one another as Jesus commanded us to do.

Activity

Think of the blessings God has given you and your family. Fill the Blessings Bucket with words and images that tell of blessings you have received. Share what is in it with your classmates. Show that you are thankful. Pray with your class, "Blessed be God for ever."

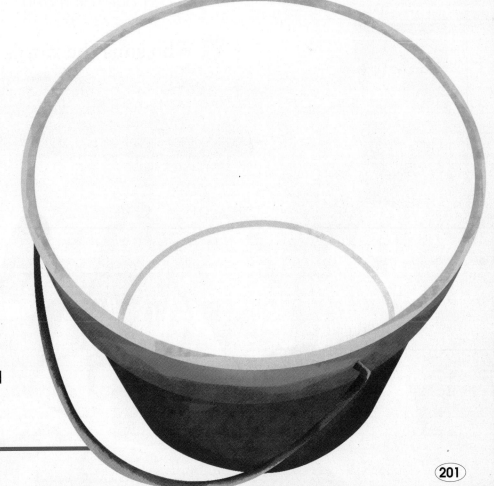

The Eucharistic Prayer

The Eucharistic Prayer is the Church's great prayer of thanksgiving. It is during this prayer that we do what Jesus did at the Last Supper the night before he died.

During the meal, Jesus took bread into his hands and said a blessing prayer. He broke the bread. Giving the bread to his disciples, Jesus said, "Take and eat. This is my body. Do this in memory of me."

Jesus took a cup of wine and gave thanks to God. Giving the cup of wine to his disciples, he said, "Drink it." They all drank from the cup. Jesus said, "This is my blood, which is poured out for many."   BASED ON LUKE 22:17–20

Who says the words of Jesus at Mass?

The Consecration

The priest takes bread and says,
"**T**AKE THIS, ALL OF YOU, AND EAT OF IT,
FOR THIS IS MY **B**ODY,
WHICH WILL BE GIVEN UP FOR YOU."

Then he takes the cup of wine and says,
"**T**AKE THIS, ALL OF YOU, AND DRINK
FROM IT, FOR THIS IS THE CHALICE
OF MY **B**LOOD, THE **B**LOOD OF THE
NEW AND ETERNAL COVENANT,
WHICH WILL BE POURED OUT FOR
YOU AND FOR MANY FOR THE
FORGIVENESS OF SINS.
DO THIS IN MEMORY OF ME"

These are called the words of consecration.
Through the words of the priest and the
power of the Holy Spirit, the bread and wine
become the Body and Blood of Christ.

At the end of the Eucharistic Prayer,
the assembly stands. We sing or say
aloud, "Amen."

❓ How are the Eucharistic Prayer and
the Last Supper alike?

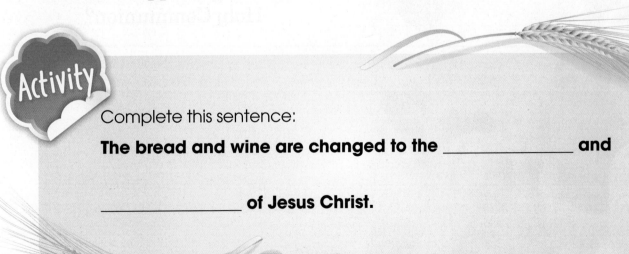

Activity

Complete this sentence:

The bread and wine are changed to the _____ **and**

_____ **of Jesus Christ.**

The Communion Rite

After we pray the Our Father and share a sign of peace, the priest invites us to come forward to receive Holy Communion. We receive the gift of Jesus himself. We receive strength to live as his disciples.

We walk in procession to receive Holy Communion. The consecrated bread is offered to us with the words, "The Body of Christ." We respond, "Amen."

The cup of consecrated wine is then offered to us. We hear the words, "The Blood of Christ." We respond, "Amen." We take the cup and drink from it.

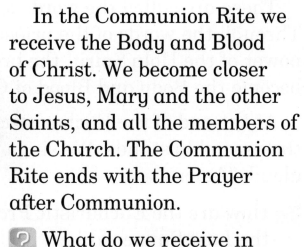

In the Communion Rite we receive the Body and Blood of Christ. We become closer to Jesus, Mary and the other Saints, and all the members of the Church. The Communion Rite ends with the Prayer after Communion.

❓ What do we receive in Holy Communion?

At Mass, you receive the gift of the Body and Blood of Christ. One way you can give thanks for the blessings God gives you is by sharing your blessings with other people.

I Follow Jesus

Activity

Sharing My Blessings

Think of how the Holy Spirit helps you share the many blessings you have been given. Write a prayer of thanks to God for all his blessings. Ask the Holy Spirit to help you share your blessings with others.

_____

_____

_____

_____

My Faith Choice

This week, I will share the blessings God has given me. I will

_____

_____.

Pray, "You have blessed me, O Lord. Teach me and help me to share my blessings. Amen."

1. At the Last Supper, Jesus gave the Church the Sacrament of the Eucharist.

2. At the celebration of the Eucharist, the bread and wine become the Body and Blood of Jesus.

3. We receive the Body and Blood of Jesus in Holy Communion.

Chapter Review

Recall

Draw a line from each of the words in the left column to the sentence it completes in the right column.

Words	Sentences
Sacrament	The _____ is the Church's great prayer of thanksgiving.
Eucharistic Prayer	At the Eucharist, we do what Jesus did at the _____.
Last Supper	The Eucharist is the _____ of the Body and Blood of Christ.

Circle Yes or No after each sentence about the Liturgy of the Eucharist

The gifts of bread and wine remind us of all God's people.   **Yes   No**

At Mass the bread and wine become the Body and Blood of Jesus.   **Yes   No**

Reflect

Why is receiving Holy Communion important?

_____

_____.

Share   Share with your class how you will give thanks to God.

Blessed Be God

Blessing prayers tell God we believe that all our blessings come from him. Learn the Mass response, "Blessed be God for ever."

Leader   God our Father, we thank you for all your blessings.

All   **Blessed be God for ever.**

Leader   For family and friends, we thank you, God, and say,

All   **Blessed be God for ever.**

Leader   For the gifts you give us to share, _____, we thank you, God, and say,

All   **Blessed be God for ever.**

Leader   And most especially, for the gift of Jesus in the Eucharist, we thank you, God, and say,

All   **Blessed be God for ever.**

With My Family

This Week . . .

In Chapter 15, "We Give Thanks," your child learned:

▶ Jesus gave the Church the Sacrament of the Eucharist at the Last Supper.

▶ During the Eucharistic Prayer at Mass, the Church remembers and does what Jesus did at the Last Supper.

▶ At Mass, the bread and wine become the Body and Blood of Jesus through the power of the Holy Spirit and the words of the priest. Jesus is really and truly present under the appearances of bread and wine.

▶ In Holy Communion, we receive the Body and Blood of Jesus.

▶ We thank God for this wonderful gift by the way we live our lives.

For more about related teachings of the Church, see the *Catechism of the Catholic Church*, 1345–1405, and the *United States Catholic Catechism for Adults*, pages 218–220.

■ Sharing God's Word

Read together Luke 22:11–20, part of the account of what happened at the Last Supper. Or read the adaptation of the story on page 202. Emphasize that at the Last Supper, Jesus gave the Church the Sacrament of the Eucharist.

■ Living as Disciples

The Christian home and family is a school of discipleship. Choose one of the following activities to do as a family, or design a similar activity of your own.

▶ This week at Mass, remind your child that what Jesus did at the Last Supper is part of the Eucharistic Prayer. After Mass, talk with your child about the Last Supper and its connection with the Mass. Discuss the importance of receiving Holy Communion.

▶ Sharing family meals together is a practical way to help your child appreciate and understand the meaning of the Eucharist. When your family shares meals together, you are sharing the gift of yourselves. Be sure to give thanks to God by praying Grace Before Meals.

■ Our Spiritual Journey

One of the effects of receiving the gift of the Eucharist in Holy Communion is living out a commitment to the poor. Practicing the spiritual discipline of almsgiving enables us to live out that grace and also to thank God for all his blessings, not only in words but also in our actions. This week, pray *"Blessed be God for ever"* at the end of each family meal prayer.

For more ideas on ways your family can live as disciples of Jesus, visit **BeMyDisciples.com**

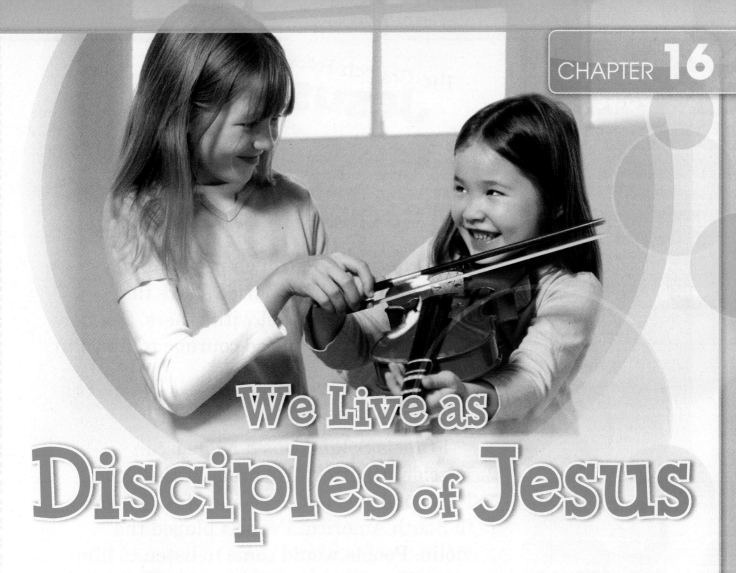

CHAPTER 16

We Live as Disciples of Jesus

? When did someone call on you to do something important?

Each day God calls on us to help him. Close your eyes and imagine you lived many years before Jesus was born. Listen to God calling on you to help him.

I heard the voice of the Lord saying,
"Whom shall I send?" . . . "Here I am;"
I said; "send me!"

ISAIAH 6:8

? What message would you share about Jesus with another?

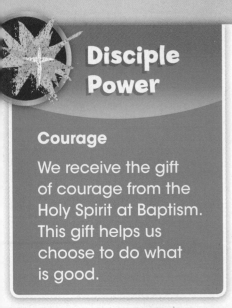

Spreading the Gospel

God continues to call on people to be missionaries. Missionaries share the message of the Gospel with others. See how these missionaries used courage to listen to God's call.

Saint Francis Solano

Francis Solano was a Franciscan missionary priest. He brought the Good News of Jesus to the people of Argentina in South America. Francis played the violin. People would come to listen to him play. Then Francis would teach them about Jesus.

Jean Donovan

Jean Donovan left her home in Ohio to go to the country of El Salvador in Central America. Jean shared God's love and showed her love especially to people who were poor. Jean ran a home for the hungry and the sick. Jean Donovan was killed by people who did not want her to be a missionary in their country.

? How did these missionaries share the Gospel message?

Saint Frances Cabrini

Frances Cabrini brought her missionary sisters from Italy to New York. They helped the sick and cared for orphans. They built schools and orphanages in the United States and South America. She became so loved by the people they called her "Mother Cabrini."

? If you were a missionary, where would you go? How would you help?

Saint Francis Solano, Saint Frances Cabrini, Jean Donovan

Activity

Living as a Missionary

Write what you think you would like most and what you think would be hardest about being a missionary.

_____

_____

_____

_____

_____

The Concluding Rites

The Concluding Rites end the celebration of the Mass. We receive God's blessing and go forth to tell others about Jesus.

Final Blessing

The priest asks for God's blessing on us. He says, "May almighty God bless you, the Father, and the Son, and the Holy Spirit."

We end Mass the same way we began. We bless ourselves with the Sign of the Cross. We respond, "Amen."

Dismissal

The word *mass* means "sending forth." What we have done at Mass, we must now do in the world. We are to be messengers of God by what we say and what we do. That is our work as disciples of Jesus.

The deacon or priest says, "Go in peace, glorifying the Lord by your life." We respond, "Thanks be to God."

? How are we to be messengers of God?

Messengers of God

You can be a missionary and messenger of God. Finish the sentences by writing what you can say or do to live your faith as a follower of Jesus.

1. If someone hurts me, I can

   _____

   _____.

2. If someone forgot to bring lunch to school, I can

   _____

   _____.

3. If someone is bullying another, I can

   _____

   _____.

4. If I hurt someone, I can

   _____

   _____.

5. If someone I know is sick, I can

   _____

   _____.

Saint Damien de Veuster

Faith Focus
What must we do to
glorify God by our lives?

Jesus Gives Us a Mission

At the Last Supper, Jesus told us how we are to glorify God. Listen to what he told his disciples.

At the Last Supper, Jesus tied a towel around his waist and poured water into a bowl. Then he washed his disciples' feet and dried them with the towel.

When he finished, Jesus said, "Do you understand what I have done for you? You call me teacher and Lord. That is who I am. If I have washed your feet, you must wash one another's feet. You must serve one another.

"Here is what you are to do. You are to love one another as I have loved you. Then everyone will know that you are my disciples." BASED ON JOHN 13:4–5, 13–14, 34–35

? What is the work that Jesus gave us to do?

Jesus showed his disciples how to glorify God by their lives. We are to love and serve one another. We are to do what he did.

We show our thanks to God when we try our very best to live as Jesus taught. When we do this we love God and people as Jesus did.

? What are ways you love and serve others?

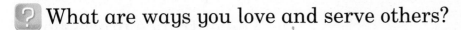

The Mission to Love

Discover our mission. Use the code to find out what we must do to love and serve the Lord.

1 = A	2 = E	3 = O

L __ V __ __ N __ __ __ N __ TH __ R
  3   2   3 2 1   3   2

__ S I H __ V __ L __ V __ D Y __ U.
1   1 2   3 2   3

The Concluding Procession

We leave the Church to do what we were sent to do. We leave together in **procession**.

Processions are prayers in action. A procession is when people prayerfully walk together. There are five processions at Mass.

1. The entrance procession at the start of Mass

2. The Gospel procession during the Liturgy of the Word

3. The procession bringing the gifts to the altar at the start of the Liturgy of the Eucharist

4. The procession to receive Holy Communion

5. The procession at the end of Mass

At the end of Mass, we are blessed and sent forth to do the work of Jesus. We are sent from the church to love and serve God and people. We know that the Eucharist gives us the strength to be disciples of Jesus.

? What is the work that Jesus gave us to do?

You can give glory to God when you live as Jesus taught. You show love to others. You can show courage and do things that are difficult because of your love for God. When you do this, you love God and serve people as Jesus did.

To Love and Serve

The Holy Spirit helps you give glory to God. Think of how you will live, love, and serve others with courage. Put a ✔ next to ways you can do this. Act out one of these ways for your class.

_____ I can help out at home.

_____ I can pray for people around the world who suffer from poverty.

_____ I can say no to fighting and arguing with my family.

_____ I can donate some of my toys to children who have less than I do.

_____ I can be a respectful listener at school.

My Faith Choice

I will glorify the Lord this week. I will

_____

_____

_____ .

Pray, "Help me show my love for you, Lord God, in all I do for others. Amen."

1. At the end of Mass we receive God's blessing to live as Jesus' disciples.

2. The dismissal sends us forth from Mass to glorify God.

3. The concluding procession reminds us that we are people sent on a mission.

Chapter Review

Recall

Write the missing words in the sentences.
Use the words below to help you.

mass	procession	love	missionaries

1. _____ teach and help poor people all over the world.

2. The word _____ means "sending forth."

3. A _____ is a prayer in action.

Number the parts of the Concluding Rites in the correct order.

____ The Concluding Procession

____ The Dismissal

____ The Final Blessing

Reflect

In what ways will you go forth to love and serve others?

_____

_____

_____

Share   Share with your class the ways that you will give glory to God this week.

Here I Am, Lord

Prayer can help us tell others about God's love.
Say this prayer with your class.

Leader Prayer can help us say, "Here I am. Send me." Therefore, let us pray.

Group 1 Loving Lord, you ask us to be your messengers.

All **"Here I am, Lord. Send me."**

Group 2 You bless and call us to love one another.

All **"Here I am, Lord. Send me."**

Group 1 You bless us and call us to serve others.

All **"Here I am, Lord. Send me."**

Group 2 Lord, whenever you call us to love and to serve, help us say,

All **"Here I am, Lord. Send me. Amen"**

With My Family

This Week . . .

In Chapter 16, "We Live as Disciples of Jesus," your child learned:

▶ The Concluding Rites end the celebration of Mass.

▶ In the Concluding Rites of the Mass, we are blessed and sent forth as messengers of the Gospel.

▶ The concluding procession alerts us to the fact that we are sent forth together and are to work together as messengers of the Gospel.

▶ Exercising courage in living as Jesus taught is an important characteristic of Jesus' disciples.

For more about related teachings of the Church, see the *Catechism of the Catholic Church*, 1333–1405 and 1822–1823; and the *United States Catholic Catechism for Adults*, pages 220–227.

■ Sharing God's Word

Read together John 13:1–15 and 33–34, the account of Jesus giving the disciples his New Commandment. Or read the adaptation of the story on page 214. Point out how Jesus calls us to love and serve others as he did.

■ Livings as Disciples

The Christian home and family is a school of discipleship. Choose one of the following activities to do as a family, or design a similar activity of your own.

▶ Review the assembly's responses to the Blessing and Dismissal of the Concluding Rites. Make sure your child knows them by heart. This will help them participate more fully and actively in the celebration of Mass.

▶ Discuss and decide how your family can glorify God by your lives; for example, by taking part in a service project of your parish or school that serves your neighborhood or local community.

■ Our Spiritual Journey

Developing the virtues can occur through human effort — dilligence, consistent practice, and courage — assisted by God's grace. In this chapter, your child was introduced to the virtue of courage. Model this virtue: help your child learn and practice it through your example. Pray this simple prayer each day with your family, "Here I am, Lord. Send me."

For more ideas on ways your family can live as disciples of Jesus, visit **BeMyDisciples.com**

Sharing God's Love

We respect the elders in our community. They may have helped to take care of children, worked to help others, and know a lot about life. Some elderly people live alone. What can you do to show them that you love them and care for them?

It is no fun to be sick. Imagine if you were stuck in bed all day every day because you were too sick to get up. Some children are very sick for a long time. How can you help cheer them up?

Some families do not have the basic things they need. They do not have enough food, clothing, or even a place to live. Places like homeless shelters try to help families who are going through hard times. How can you help?

WE REACH OUT TO PEOPLE

Many people need our love and support. We can share what we have with people who are older, who are sick, and who are poor.

Making Connections

Jesus told us that when we care for people who are elderly, sick, and homeless, we are caring for him. We are to share what we have with those who are in need.

with Math and Science

Your class is going to collect money to donate to the homeless shelter for families in your town. Use a chart to calculate how much your class collected in one week. Then estimate how much you can collect in four weeks.

with Language Arts

Think of someone you know that may be sick or find out the name of someone in your school who is sick. You can show you care by making a get-well card. Think about the picture and words you want on the outside cover. Inside, write a cheery message. Be sure to sign your name.

with Social Studies

Talk with your grandparents or neighbors who are elderly. Ask about what life was like when they were your age. Use a chart to help you find out what is the same between your life and their lives when they were young. Then find out what is different. Thank them for sharing their wisdom with you.

Faith Action

Show Jesus' love to those in need. Choose a project to do on your own to help someone who is elderly, who is sick, or who needs help. The project that I choose is _____

_____

_____ .

Unit 4 Review

Name _____

A. Choose the Best Word

Fill in the blanks to complete each of the sentences.
Use the words from the word bank.

| Word | Mass | Amen | Last Supper | assembly |

1. The _____ is the most important celebration of the Church.

2. We call the people God gathers to celebrate Mass the _____.

3. The Liturgy of the _____ is the first main part of the Mass.

4. In the Liturgy of the Eucharist, the Church does what Jesus did at the _____.

5. When we receive the consecrated bread and wine in Holy Communion, we say, "_____."

B. Show What You Know

Match the terms in Column A with their meaning in Column B.

Column A

1. The Introductory Rites

2. knowledge

3. Eucharist

4. Eucharistic Prayer

5. love

Column B

____ A. Sacrament of the Body and Blood of Christ.

____ B. the greatest of all virtues.

____ C. rites gather us and prepare us to worship God.

____ D. virtue that helps us to better hear and understand the meaning of God's Word.

____ E. Church's great prayer of thanksgiving.

C. Connect with Scripture

What was your favorite story about Jesus in this unit?
Draw something that happened in the story.
Tell your class about it.

D. Be a Disciple

1. *What Saint or holy person did you enjoy hearing about in this unit? Write the name here. Tell your class what this person did to follow Jesus.*

_____

_____

2. *What can you do to be a good disciple of Jesus?*

_____

_____

Blessed by God

Jesus was a wonderful teacher. One day Jesus taught his followers eight special ways to live called the Beatitudes. *Beatitude* means "blessing."

Jesus told the crowds that God will bless, or take care of the people who have the most needs. He will also bless those who help others and care for them.

God's Kingdom will belong to those who do what is right.

BASED ON MATTHEW 5:3–10

What I Know

What is something you already know about these faith concepts?

Being Holy

_____

_____

Being Happy

_____

_____

Ten Commandments

_____

_____

*Put an **X** next to the faith words you know. Put a **?** next to the faith words you need to learn more about.*

_____ grace   _____ courage   _____ false witness

_____ honor   _____ rabbi   _____ justice

_____ Great Commandment

What do you know about the Golden Rule in the Bible?

_____

A Question I Have

What question would you like to ask about living
the Ten Commandments?

_____

_____

Chapter 17

In God's Image

? Who are some of the people who love you? What are some of the ways they show you they love you?

Listen to find out how much God loves you:

See how very much God the Father loves us.

He calls us his own children!

BASED ON 1 JOHN 3:1

? What do you think it means that God calls you his child?

Kindness

We are kind when we do things that show we care. We are kind when we treat other people as we want to be treated.

The Church Follows **Jesus**

The Little Flower

Thérèse of Lisieux was proud to be a child of God. Thérèse tried her best to do little things well.

Thérèse wrote a story about her life. When she was a young girl, she grew flowers and took care of her pet birds. She treated everyone with kindness. She wrote about the little things that we can do each day out of love.

When Thérèse was fifteen she became a religious sister. She called herself God's "little flower." She wanted to give glory to God in small ways, just as flowers do.

Saint Thérèse of Lisieux is also called Saint Thérèse of the Child Jesus. She is also known as The Little Flower. Her feast day is October 1.

❓ What are some of the little things that you can do to show respect for God and others?

Little Kindnesses

Saint Thérèse of the Child Jesus knew that the little kindnesses we do matter. Look at the many little kindnesses. Choose a different one to do each day this week. Check the ones you choose.

- ❏ Tell your parents you love them.

- ❏ Smile at everyone today.

- ❏ Bring one of your toys to a homeless shelter.

- ❏ Do a chore without being asked.

- ❏ Let your brother or sister play with your toys.

- ❏ Make and send a card to a friend.

- ❏ Sing someone a song.

- ❏ Pick up litter.

- ❏ Forgive someone who has hurt you.

- ❏ Tell a joke.

- ❏ Give a hug.

- ❏ Surprise someone with a little gift.

- ❏ Be polite.

- ❏ Make someone laugh.

- ❏ Offer to help at home or at school.

- ❏ Tell someone, "You're doing great!"

Faith Focus
How are we honored
and blessed by God?

Faith Words
▶ **honor**
To honor someone
is to treat them with
kindness, respect,
and love.

We Are Holy

The Bible teaches that God creates us
to be holy and gives every person a great
honor. To honor someone is to treat that
person with kindness, respect, and love.
The first book of the Bible says:

God created man in his image;

in the divine image he created him;

male and female he created them.

God blessed them, . . .

GENESIS 1:27–28

The Book of Psalms sings of this honor
and blessing.

You have blessed us, O Lord, with glory
and honor.

BASED ON PSALM 8:6

We are holy because we
are made in God's image.
We are called to be like
God who is holy.

We are honored because
God shares his life with us.
We are blessed to be God's
own children.

[?] As God's children, how
are we to honor God?

Jesus and the Children

Jesus taught us to honor God, ourselves, and other people. He taught us to treat people with kindness, respect, and love. Jesus taught us to honor all people as children of God.

Jesus' disciples were wondering who would be the greatest in heaven. So Jesus picked up a little child and said to his disciples, "Become like this child and love God as this child loves him. If you do, God will welcome you into heaven."

BASED ON MATTHEW 18:1–4

Catholics Believe

Fruits of the Holy Spirit

The Bible names some signs that show when we are trying to live as children of God. Three of these signs are joy, generosity, and kindness. We call these signs Fruits of the Holy Spirit.

Activity Imagine that you are one of the children in the picture. Act out the scene with a partner. Write what you would say to Jesus.

Jesus Is Our Teacher

The disciples of Jesus honored him in many ways. They honored and respected him as their teacher. In Jesus' time to call someone "Teacher" was a sign of great honor and respect.

Everything Jesus said and did gave honor to his Father. Jesus' disciples listened to him carefully. They did as he said. They believed that Jesus would teach them how to live as children of God.

The disciples learned from Jesus. He taught them about himself:

"I am the way and the truth and the life.

JOHN 14:6

Jesus taught the disciples that he would lead them to God. Jesus will lead us to God.

? What does Jesus teach us how to do?

Jesus is our Teacher too. He is the way, the truth, and the life. We listen to him. We learn from him. We try our best to live as Jesus taught.

? Why do you think Jesus is our teacher too?

Following Jesus

Follow each path to Jesus. Ask Jesus to teach you to live as a child of God.

Way

Life

Truth

233

Faith Focus
How do we show we
are children of God?

Faith Words
grace
Grace is the gift of
God sharing his life
with us. It is also God
helping us to make
good choices to live as
children of God.

Making Good Choices

Jesus taught us how to make good choices. We show that we are proud to be children of God when we make good choices. We show that we are proud and honored to call Jesus "Teacher."

We live as children of God when we make good choices. We show that we are trying our best to live as children of God. We grow in kindness. We love God, ourselves, and other people as Jesus did.

God the Holy Spirit helps us to make good choices. He gives us his **grace**, or help, to make good choices. When we make good choices, we grow as children of God.

? Who has helped you make good choices to live as a child of God? Have you helped others?

The Holy Spirit helps you to make choices. He helps you to be kind. He helps you be fair. When you are kind and fair, you show that you are proud to be a child of God.

I Follow Jesus

Activity

Living as a Child of God

Write some words of kindness that you say. Then write acts of kindness that you do to show that you are a child of God.

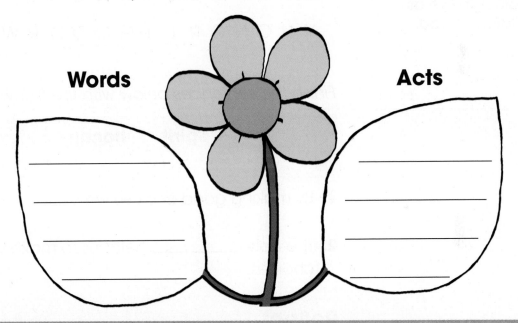

Words

Acts

My Faith Choice

This week, I will surprise someone with this act of kindness. I will

_____

_____

Pray, "Father, thank you for loving me so much. Help me with your grace to make good choices. Help me to grow as your child. Amen."

Chapter Review

Recall

Find and circle the words hidden in the puzzle.

respect	kindness	good	love
follow	choices	honor	faith

R E S P E C T L K I N D N E S S

O F O L L O W P N Z T F A I T H

C H O I C E S T R W L O V E P T

Y H O N O R L I G O O D R W Z A

Finish the sentences below with the following words.

Spirit   honor

1. By making good choices we _____ God.

2. The Holy _____ helps us to make wise
choices.

Reflect

*What are the ways you will choose to live as a child
of God? Use the words from the puzzle to help you
decide.*

_____

_____

Share | Write down an act of kindness you
will do for a friend or family member
this week.

May God Bless Us

Pray this prayer to ask God to bless your class.
Ask him to help you live as children of God.

Leader Father, we ask your blessing on us.

All **Father, we are your children.**

Leader Guide us to choose what is good and to do your will.

All **Father, we are your children.**

Leader *(Ask each child to come forward for a blessing. Place a hand on the child's head.)*
May God bless you and keep you.

All **Amen.**

Leader Together, let us pray that we may live as children of God.

All **Yes or no?**
Stay or go?
Will or won't?
Do or don't?
Choose what's best
And we'll be blest.
Make good choices.
God rejoices!

With My Family

This Week . . .

In Chapter 17, "In God's Image," your child learned:

▶ We are to honor and respect all people. Every person has the dignity of being a child of God, because we are created in the image and likeness of God.

▶ Jesus is our Teacher. He showed us how to live as children of God. He said, "I am the way and the truth, and the life. I will lead you to God" (Based on John 14:6).

▶ We honor and respect Jesus as our Teacher when we try our best to live as he taught.

▶ We grow in the virtue of kindness when we try to have all our words and actions show respect for God, for other people, and for ourselves.

For more about related teachings of the Church, see the *Catechism of the Catholic Church*, 1699–1756 and 1996–2016, and the *United States Catholic Catechism for Adults*, pages 307–309, 324–331, 351–354.

■ Sharing God's Word

Read together Mark 10:13–16, "Jesus and the Children." Emphasize that Jesus taught us to love God as children do and to respect all people as children of God.

■ Living as Disciples

The Christian home and family form a school of discipleship. Choose one of the following activities to do as a family, or design a similar activity of your own.

▶ Notice when your child makes good choices. Compliment him or her and point out how the Church helps us make good choices. Praise your child for trying his or her best to live as Jesus taught.

▶ Saint Thérèse of the Child Jesus focused on doing the little things in life out of love. Decide together how your family can live this week as Saint Thérèse did and do the kind things, that are part of daily life, out of love.

■ Our Spiritual Journey

The *Story of a Soul,* the autobiography of Saint Thérèse of the Child Jesus reveals to us the depth of her spirituality. Her childlike simplicity is appealing to young children. Pray these words from a poem of Saint Thérèse this week: "Come reign within my heart, smile tenderly on me, today, dear Lord, today."

For more ideas on ways your family can live as disciples of Jesus, visit **BeMyDisciples.com**

Chapter 18

We Live as Children of God

? What is something that you have learned from a teacher?

Here is a prayer from the Bible. Listen carefully to what the person is asking God:

Make known to me your ways, LORD;
　　teach me your paths.
Guide me in your truth and teach me,
　　for you are God my savior.

PSALM 25:4–5a

? What would you like to ask God to teach you?

Fortitude

Fortitude is another word for courage. Fortitude helps us to stay strong, to do our best, and to do what is right and good when it is hard to do so. The Holy Spirit gives us the gift of fortitude to live the way that God wants us to live.

The Church Follows **Jesus**

Saint Pedro

Pedro Calungsod lived on the island of Cebu in the Philippines. When he was a teenager, he played sports. He had a job as a carpenter. Pedro became a religion teacher or a catechist. He taught others about God and his Son, Jesus.

Pedro left his home to become a missionary to people who did not know about God. Pedro needed courage to do this work. He had to cross over high mountains. He had to go through deep jungles. It was not easy, but Pedro did not give up. He wanted to do his best to teach people about the Holy Trinity.

The people of the Philippines honor Pedro each year with a festival. The Church honors Pedro by calling him Saint Pedro Calungsod.

? How did Saint Pedro live the virtue of fortitude, or courage?

Pope Benedict XVI and the Church honored Saint Pedro by calling him a Saint in the year 2012. We celebrate the feast day of Saint Pedro on April 2.

Today many teachers live the virtue of fortitude. They share the Good News about Jesus and live as a child of God.

? What are some ways you live the virtue of fortitude, or courage?

Activity

Honoring Teachers

Look at the pictures. How are the teachers sharing Jesus' message of love?

Write the name of someone who teaches you.

_____

Write what the teacher teaches. Tell how this teacher shares Jesus' love with you and others.

_____

_____

_____

A Different Teacher

There were many teachers of God's Law in Jesus' time. They were called rabbis. Remember, *rabbi* means "teacher."

Crowds of people followed Jesus everywhere. People wanted to learn about God from him. They said that they had never before heard a teacher like Jesus.

Jesus was different from the other rabbis. All of the religious teachers of Jesus' time relied on other teachers. They needed other respected teachers to prove that their teaching was right, but not Jesus.

Jesus taught about God on his own. He is God, the Second Person of the Holy Trinity Jesus said,

"Whoever has seen me has seen the Father."   JOHN 14:9

Jesus also taught with great kindness and mercy. Jesus said,

"Once you learned that if someone hurts you, you can hurt him back. But now I say, be kind, forgive, and love your enemies."

BASED ON MATTHEW 5:43–44

What made Jesus' teaching different?

The teachings of Jesus came from God. Jesus said,

"My teaching is not my own but it is from the one who sent me."

JOHN 7:16

Jesus' teaching took God's Law and put it into people's hearts. Jesus taught us rules for living and ways to live together. Never before was there a teacher like Jesus.

? Who sent Jesus? What are the ways you live the rules that Jesus taught us?

Activity

The Teachings of Jesus

Learn what Jesus says about following his teaching. Cross out Q, X, and Z in the puzzle.

Z W Q X H O Q Z E Q X V Z E X R Z
L X O Q V X E S Z M Z E W Q I X L L
Q F Z X O X L X L X Z O Z W X M Q Y
Z T Q E X Q A Z C Q H Z X I Z N Q G

BASED ON JOHN 14:23

Complete the sentence with the words you found in the puzzle.

Jesus said to his disciples,

_____

_____

Faith Focus
What did Jesus teach about God's Commandments?

Faith Words
▶ **Great Commandment**
The Great Commandment is to love God above all else and to love others as we love ourselves.

Jesus Teaches

One day, a teacher of the Law came to Jesus and asked,

"Teacher, which commandment in the law is the greatest?" He said to him, "You shall love the Lord, your God, with all your heart, with all your soul, and with all your mind. This is the greatest and the first commandment. The second is like it: You shall love your neighbor as yourself. The whole law and the prophets depend on these two commandments."

MATTHEW 22:36–39

Jesus named two Commandments. We are to love God above all else. We are to love our neighbor as ourselves. Together both Commandments make up one **Great Commandment.**

❓ How do you show love to God and to others?

Loving God and Others

Read the Scripture verses again. Name the two parts of the Great Commandment.

_____

_____

_____

Write a list of ways you can live the Great Commandment.

Ways I Can Love God

_____

_____

_____

_____

Ways I Can Love Others

_____

_____

_____

_____

Faith-Filled People

Saint Peter

Peter was one of Jesus' twelve Apostles. He was the first one to recognize that Jesus is the Savior. After he rose from the dead, Jesus asked Peter to care for the Church and all its members. Peter was the first Pope. His feast day is June 29.

The Great Commandment

The Great Commandment sums up all of God's Laws. The first part of the Great Commandment teaches that God is the center of our lives. It teaches us to love God above all else.

We live the first part of the Great Commandment in many ways. We show our love for God when we honor and respect God in all we do and say. We show our love for God when we pray.

The second part of the Great Commandment teaches us to treat others as we like to be treated. We live this part of the Great Commandment in many ways. We are to respect and honor all people as ourselves. We respect and honor all people when we help them care for their belongings. We respect and honor people when we treat them fairly.

? How are the people in the pictures showing love for God and for one another?

Because God loves you, you can love others. The Holy Spirit helps you to live the Great Commandment. You can love God above all else. You can love others as you love yourself.

I Follow Jesus

Activity

Teaching Others

Pretend that you are teaching a class about the Great Commandment. Draw two pictures to show what it means.

Love God	Love Others

My Faith Choice

I will show fortitude and live the Great Commandment. This week, I will

_____

_____

 Pray, "Loving God, always be my teacher. Teach me the way to love you and others with all my heart, soul, and mind. Amen."

Chapter Review

Recall

Write one word that names whom the Great Commandment tells you to love in each heart.

Match the words to their meanings.

Words

_____ **1.** rabbi

_____ **2.** courage

_____ **3.** Great Commandment

Meanings

a. sums up all of God's Laws

b. the word that means teacher

c. another name for fortitude

Reflect

Write about one of Jesus' teachings that has helped you. Tell how it has helped you.

_____

_____

_____

_____

Share — Tell a family member about how you live the Great Commandment.

An Act of Love

God is with us all day long. Take time each day to tell God you love him.

Leader We gather to hear God's Word of love.

Reader *God is love. If we are loving, we are friends with God, and God will be friends with us for ever.*

Based on 1 John 4:16

The word of the Lord.

All **Thanks be to God.**

Leader Let us tell God that we want to live the Great Commandment.

All **O my God,**
I love you above all things.
I love you with my whole heart and soul.
I love my neighbor as myself because of my love for you.

Leader O God, give us the fortitude to keep your Great Commandment of love.

All **Amen.**

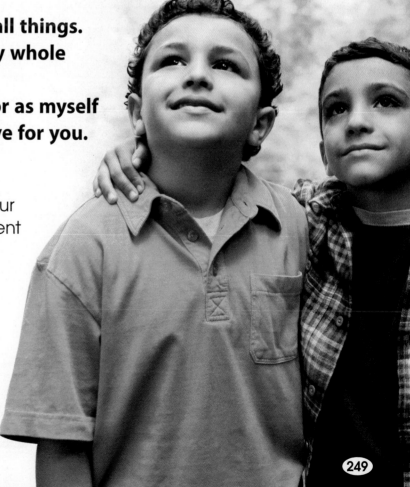

With My Family

This Week . . .

In Chapter 18, "We Live as Children of God," your child learned:

▶ Jesus taught that the heart of God's Law is the Great Commandment.

▶ The driving spirit of all God's Laws is summarized in two Commandments, namely, to love God and love others as yourself.

▶ The virtue of fortitude or courage helps us live the Great Commandment.

For more about related teachings of the Church, see the *Catechism of the Catholic Church*, 2052–2055, 2083, and 2196, and the *United States Catholic Catechism for Adults*, pages 307–309.

■ Sharing God's Word

Read together Matthew 22:34–40, Jesus' teaching on the Great Commandment, or read the adaptation of the story on page 244. Emphasize that the Great Commandment has two connected parts: love God, and love your neighbor as yourself. This commandment sums up what is at the heart and purpose of God's Laws.

■ Living as Disciples

The Christian home and family form a school of discipleship. Choose one of the following activities to do as a family, or design a similar activity of your own.

▶ Create a large heart out of poster paper. Write the Great Commandment within the heart. Display the heart where it will serve as a reminder to the whole family to live the Great Commandment.

▶ The Great Commandment tells us to treat others as we would like to be treated. Talk about some of the practical ways that your family is living this part of the Great Commandment. Encourage your children to ask themselves at bedtime how well they lived the Great Commandment that day.

■ Our Spiritual Journey

The moral virtues give us strength to live the moral life, but these virtues are acquired through deliberate effort and much practice. The virtue of fortitude helps us keep the Great Commandment—no simple task. Following the Great Commandment means more than embracing a teaching of the faith. It means embracing the Teacher, Jesus himself—or, to be exact, allowing Jesus to embrace us. Help your child pray the Act of Love on page 249. Pray together: *Give us the fortitude to keep your Great Commandment.*

For more ideas on ways your family can live as disciples of Jesus, visit **BeMyDisciples.com**

Chapter 19

We Love God

In the Bible, God tells why he gives us rules. Listen to what the writer of this psalm discovered.

Happy are those who obey God's rules.
Happy are those who keep God's laws.
They are on their way to God.

BASED ON PSALM 119:1–3

? Why does obeying God's rules make a person happy?

Obedience

Authority is a gift from God. God gives people authority to help us follow God's Laws. People in authority, such as parents and grandparents, teachers and principals, priests and bishops, deserve respect. The virtue of obedience gives us strength to honor and respect people in authority.

The Church Follows Jesus

Saint Benedict

Many years ago, a boy named Benedict learned the importance of good rules. At school, he saw that not obeying rules made people very unhappy.

When Benedict was older, he went to the countryside to live on his own. He spent each day praying and reading God's Word. Soon, families sent their sons to Benedict to learn about prayer and the Bible.

Benedict decided to build a monastery where men could live, work, and pray together. His monastery became a place where everyone obeyed the same rules.

Benedict's rules helped the men and others learn how to pray, to love God's Word, and to work together. Today, we call Benedict's rules "The Rule of Saint Benedict." These rules continue to help many people live holy and happy lives today.

? Which rules would help people in your family live happy and holy lives?

Rules Rule

Rules are important. You can't play a game without rules. Rules let you play fairly and have fun. What rules do you have in your classroom? Why are these rules important for everyone?

Write one rule you have to follow at home. Tell a partner why this rule is helpful.

Write one rule you have to follow at school. Tell a partner why this rule helps the students in your school.

Faith Words

▶ **Ten Commandments**
The Ten
Commandments are
the laws that God gave
Moses. They teach us
to live as God's people.
They help us live happy
and holy lives.

God's Rules

Long ago, God chose Moses to lead his
people out of slavery in Egypt. God's people
were not living as God wanted them to
live. God called Moses to the top of a high
mountain. God spoke to Moses and gave
him the **Ten Commandments**.

God told Moses that he loved the people.
The Ten Commandments are God's rules to
help all people live happy and holy lives.

The Ten Commandments remind people
to honor God above everything else. They
tell people to rest and pray on the Lord's
Day. They ask people to obey parents and
to keep away from telling lies or stealing.
The Commandments also say not to hurt
other people or be jealous of them.

❓ How do the Ten Commandments help
us live as God wants us to live?

The Ten Commandments are God's Laws for all people. The first three of the Ten Commandments teach us ways we are to love and honor God. The next seven of the Ten Commandments show us the ways we are to love and honor all people. All the Ten Commandments teach us how to live as children of God.

? What do the Ten Commandments teach us?

Activity

Living as Children of God

Write one way you show your love and honor for God.

Write one way you show your love and honor for people.

Catholics Believe

The Bishop's Motto

A motto is a short saying. For example, the motto of the Benedictines is "Work and Pray." Cardinal Donald Wuerl, Archbishop of Washington, DC, uses a motto to describe his work. He chose as his motto, "Thy Kingdom Come."

Keeping God First

The First, Second, and Third Commandments name ways that we are to honor and love God.

First Commandment

1. I am the Lord your God: you shall not have strange gods before me.

The First Commandment tells us there is only one God. We are to worship God alone. We are to have faith in God, to hope in him, and to love him more than all else.

Second Commandment

2. You shall not take the name of the Lord your God in vain.

The Second Commandment teaches us that God's name is holy. We are to honor God's name. We are always to speak it with respect and love. We are also to show respect for holy people, places, and things.

Third Commandment

3. Remember to keep holy the Lord's Day.

The Third Commandment teaches us that we are to keep Sunday as the Lord's Day. Each Sunday, Catholics have the responsibility to gather to celebrate the Eucharist. We thank and praise God for his goodness to us.

 What are some ways you can keep the first three Commandments?

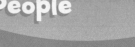
Activity

Honoring God

Use the words in the word bank to find actions that show how to follow the first three of the Ten Commandments. Find and circle each action in the puzzle.

BELIEVE   OBEY   PRAY   REST   WORSHIP   HONOR

Faith Words
proverbs
Proverbs are short sayings that help us to make good choices to follow the Ten Commandments.

Wise Sayings to Live By

The writers of the Bible collected many wise sayings to help us follow God's Law. These wise sayings are called **proverbs**. They help us choose to follow the Ten Commandments. You can read them in the Book of Proverbs in the Old Testament.

These proverbs help us show our love for God.

Trust God with all your heart.
Do not think you always have the answers.
In everything you do, keep God in mind.
God will show you the right way.

BASED ON PROVERBS 3:5–6

Honor God with the best you have.
God will take good care of you.

BASED ON PROVERBS 3:9–10

How do these proverbs help you love God and live as a child of God?

258

The Holy Spirit will always help you to make wise choices. He will give you the grace to obey the Ten Commandments. He will help you make choices to live a happy and holy life.

I Follow **Jesus**

Activity

Advice for My Family

What good advice can you give your family to help all of you love and honor God? Write your advice here and share it with them.

My Faith Choice

This week, I will show my love for God. I will

_____

_____

 Pray, "Loving God, I am happy to obey your Commandments. Help me grow in love more and more each day. Amen."

1. God gave us the Ten Commandments to teach us to live happy and holy lives.

2. The first three of the Ten Commandments teach us to love and honor God.

3. Proverbs are wise sayings that help us to love God and to live happy and holy lives.

Chapter Review

Recall

Use the words in the box to complete the sentences.

three	Proverbs	Ten

1. God gave us the _____ Commandments.

2. The first _____ Commandments tell us ways to love and honor God.

3. _____ help us show our love for God.

Color the circle next to the best word for each sentence.

4. We love _____ above all else.
   ○ people   ○ God   ○ creation

5. We respect and honor God's _____.
   ○ land   ○ face   ○ name

6. We keep holy the _____ Day.
   ○ Lord's   ○ Church's   ○ family's

Reflect

What can we learn from Saint Benedict?

_____

_____

Share — Share with your class some of the rules that you try to follow when playing with others.

Come, Holy Spirit

The Holy Spirit helps you keep God's Commandments.
Learn to sign the prayer "Come, Holy Spirit."

Come

Holy Spirit

Group 1   O Holy Spirit, you are our helper and guide. Give us your grace to live the Ten Commandments.

All   *Sign and say: "Come, Holy Spirit."*

Group 2   Holy Spirit, teach and help us to love God above all else.

All   *Sign and say: "Come, Holy Spirit."*

Group 1   Holy Spirit, teach us and help us to use God's name with loving care.

All   *Sign and say: "Come, Holy Spirit."*

Group 2   Holy Spirit, teach us and help us to keep the Lord's Day holy.

All   *Sign and say: "Come, Holy Spirit."*

With My Family

This Week . . .

In Chapter 19, "We Love God," your child learned:

▶ The Ten Commandments guide us in living happy and holy lives.

▶ The first three of the Ten Commandments name ways that we are to love and honor God.

▶ Proverbs in the Bible are short wise sayings that help us to follow God's Law and to live happy and holy lives.

▶ The virtue of obedience strengthens us to show honor to those who have authority. Authority is a gift from God that he gives people to help us live his Law.

For more about related teachings of the Church, see the *Catechism of the Catholic Church* "First Commandment" (2083–2136), "Second Commandment" (2142–2165), "Third Commandment" (2168–2188 and 2194), and the *United States Catholic Catechism for Adults*, pages 341–369.

■ Sharing God's Word

Read together Exodus 20:1–3, 7–17. Emphasize that the Ten Commandments are God's Laws. Talk about how the Ten Commandments help us to live holy and happy lives.

■ Living as Disciples

The Christian home and family is a school of discipleship. Grow in your love of God together. Choose one of the following activities to do as a family, or design a similar activity of your own.

▶ Make prayer rocks to carry in your pockets. Use them as reminders to set aside time to pray often throughout the day. When you put your hand into your pocket, you will be reminded to pray. You will also be reminded that God is always with you.

▶ Point out and compliment your child when he or she is obedient. Share ways that you, too, are obedient to others. Help your child see that being obedient is showing respect for those in proper authority.

■ Our Spiritual Journey

Remember the Gospel story of Martha and Mary (Luke 10:38–42). It is a story of balancing work and prayer in our daily lives. It is a story about going about our daily lives keeping God at the center of our lives, just as Saint Benedict taught in his Rule. Invite the Holy Spirit to help you rediscover this balance! Pray together as a family, "*Come, Holy Spirit, fill our hearts with your love.*"

For more ideas on ways your family can live as disciples of Jesus, visit **BeMyDisciples.com**

Chapter 20

We Love Others

? How do you like other people to treat you?

Listen to what Jesus says about how we are to treat others.

Jesus told his disciples, "Treat other people the same way you want them to treat you." BASED ON MATTHEW 7:12

This is called the Golden Rule.

? Why is this a good rule?

The Church Follows **Jesus**

Justice

We practice justice when we do our very best to always be fair to others.

Caring for Others

Vincent de Paul lived the Golden Rule. He took care of people who were sick. He gave clothes and food to people who had no money. He helped people to find jobs and to build homes.

Vincent treated others as he wanted to be treated. He is a Saint of the Church. The Church celebrates the feast day of Saint Vincent de Paul on September 27.

Today, people in Catholic parishes live the Golden Rule as Vincent de Paul did. They are members of the St. Vincent de Paul Society. They live the virtues of charity and justice. They are helping to build a kind and fair world.

❓ How does your school live the Golden Rule?

People who live the Ten Commandments live the Golden Rule. They help to build a kind and fair world. They treat people with respect. They know that all people are children of God.

? What is the Golden Rule?

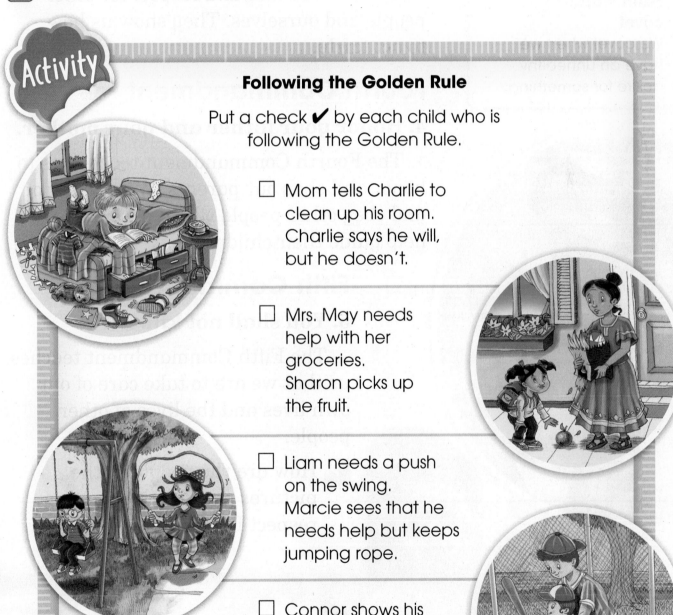

Activity

Following the Golden Rule

Put a check ✔ by each child who is following the Golden Rule.

☐ Mom tells Charlie to clean up his room. Charlie says he will, but he doesn't.

☐ Mrs. May needs help with her groceries. Sharon picks up the fruit.

☐ Liam needs a push on the swing. Marcie sees that he needs help but keeps jumping rope.

☐ Connor shows his little sister how to hit a homerun.

Faith Focus
How do the Fourth through the Tenth Commandments help people to love and respect other people and themselves?

Faith Words
covet
We covet when we have an unhealthy desire for something.

Living the Golden Rule

The first three Commandments teach us how we are to love and honor God. The seven other Commandments help us to follow the Golden Rule. These rules help us to show our love and respect for other people and ourselves. They show us how to act fairly.

Fourth Commandment

4. Honor your father and your mother.

The Fourth Commandment teaches us to honor and obey our parents. We also honor and obey other people whom parents ask to help guide their children.

Fifth Commandment

5. You shall not kill.

The Fifth Commandment teaches us that we are to take care of our own lives and the lives of other people.

[?] How are the people in the pictures showing love and respect for others?

Sixth and Ninth Commandments

6. You shall not commit adultery.

9. You shall not covet your neighbor's wife.

These two Commandments teach us that we are to respect our own bodies and the bodies of other people. We are not to let people touch us in the wrong way. We are to help families live happy and holy lives.

 What are some ways that you can help your family live happy and holy lives?

Activity

Respecting Others and Self

Finish the sentences. Tell how you can follow the Golden Rule and show love and respect for others and yourself.

I can show love and respect for my parents and family by

_____

_____.

I can show love and respect for my teachers by

_____

_____.

I can show love and respect for myself by

_____

_____.

Faith Focus
How do the Seventh, Eighth, and Tenth Commandments help us to live as children of God?

Faith Vocabulary
false witness
Giving false witness means telling lies.

Seventh Commandment

You shall not steal.

The Seventh Commandment teaches us to respect the property of other people. We are not to steal or cheat. When we want to use something that belongs to someone else, we are to ask permission. We are to return the things that we borrow in good condition.

Eighth Commandment

You shall not bear false witness against your neighbor.

The Eighth Commandment teaches that we are to be honest and truthful. We are not to lie. To bear **false witness** means to lie.

Tenth Commandment

You shall not covet your neighbor's goods.

The Tenth Commandment tells us not to be jealous of other people or their things. We are also to use food, water, and other things of creation fairly. We are to share our blessings as gifts from God.

How do the Seventh, Eighth, and Tenth Commandments help you live the Golden Rule?

Jesus taught his followers that they are to obey and live the Ten Commandments. When we live these Commandments, we are living holy lives. When we live the Ten Commandments, we will find happiness. We are living as children of God.

? What is one way we can choose to live holy lives?

Activity

Choosing a Commandment

Read the story below. Then write how the Ten Commandments will help the children make good choices.

Mrs. Andrada has planted beautiful spring flowers. Asad and Chelsea decide it is too far to walk to the playground, so they begin to kick around the ball near Mrs. Andrada's yard. What do the Ten Commandments teach that will help Asad and Chelsea know what to do while they are playing?

_____

_____

_____

_____

Share with the Poor

Jesus calls us to love and honor God and to respect one another. In this story, Jesus teaches us to do more than just to obey the Ten Commandments.

One day a man came to Jesus and asked, "Teacher, what must I do to get to heaven?"

Jesus said to the man, "You shall obey the Ten Commandments."

The man told Jesus, "I have always followed all these rules."

Looking at the man Jesus said to him, "There is one more thing you need to do. Give what you have to the poor. Then, come, follow me."

The man was very surprised at Jesus' answer. The man could not do it. He went away sad.

BASED ON MARK 10:17–22

? How does your school or parish help the poor? How can you help?

When you live the Ten Commandments, you are living as a child of God. You are building a kind and fair world. When you keep the Golden Rule and share with the poor, you are doing even more. You are living as a disciple of Jesus.

I Follow **Jesus**

Activity

My Faith Choice

I will keep the Ten Commandments this week. I will do more, as Jesus asked. I will

_____

_____.

 Pray, "Holy Spirit, teach me and help me to keep the Commandments. I want to honor you, be fair to others, and do even more. Amen."

1. People who live the Ten Commandments help to build a kind and fair world.

2. The Fourth through the Tenth Commandments teach us to love, honor, and respect other people and ourselves.

3. Jesus calls us to follow him by keeping the Ten Commandments and the Golden Rule and by doing even more.

Chapter Review

Recall

Circle Yes if a sentence is true. Circle No if a sentence is not true.

1. The Fourth through the Tenth Commandments show us how to honor, respect, and love God.   **Yes   No**

2. The Fourth Commandment is "Treat other people the same way you want them to treat you."   **Yes   No**

3. The Fourth through the Tenth Commandments show us how to follow the Golden Rule and to build a kind and fair world.   **Yes   No**

4. The Sixth and Ninth Commandments teach us that we are to respect our own bodies and the bodies of other people.   **Yes   No**

5. Jesus' followers should do more than just obey the Ten Commandments.   **Yes   No**

Reflect

Reread the Scripture story on page 270. What is Jesus asking us to do in our lives today?

_____

_____.

Share   Share with your class how you can live the Golden Rule and do even more.

Trust in the Lord!

At Baptism, we receive the grace to live God's Commandments. Pray this prayer. Tell God you will try your best to live as a follower of his Son, Jesus Christ.

Leader   Remember the Lord's teachings. Keep his laws with all your heart.

All   **Lord, teach us your laws.**

Leader   God, help us to always honor you.

All   **Lord, teach us your laws.**

Leader   God, help us to always treat others with love and respect.

All   **Lord, teach us your laws.**

Leader   Help us to love others as ourselves.

All   **Lord, teach us your laws.**

Leader   Help us to give to the poor and to do even more as Jesus asks.

All   **Lord, teach us your laws.**

Leader   Trust in the Lord with all your heart. The Lord will lead you on a straight path.

All   **Lord, we will always trust in you. Amen.**

With My Family

This Week . . .

In Chapter 20, "We Love Others," your child learned:

▶ The Fourth through the Tenth Commandments name ways that we are to love, honor, and respect other people, ourselves, and all of God's creation.

▶ The Golden Rule summarizes the Fourth through the Tenth Commandments.

▶ Jesus taught that we are to do more than just obey the Ten Commandments. We are to share our blessings with the poor.

▶ The Ten Commandments help us live as children of God. They guide us to build a kind and fair world. They help us prepare for the coming of the Kingdom of God.

▶ People who live the virtue of justice work to build a kind and fair world.

For more about related teachings of the Church, see the *Catechism of the Catholic Church*, 2196–2246, 2258–2317, 2331–2391, 2401–2449, 2464–2503, 2514–2527, 2534–2550, and the *United States Catholic Catechism for Adults,* pages 375–455.

■ Sharing God's Word

Read together Mark 10:17–22, Jesus' teaching on doing more than just obeying the Ten Commandments. As a family, discuss what more your family can do to act as Jesus' disciples and follow him. Name ways your family can build a just and kind world.

■ Living as Disciples

The Christian home and family is a school of discipleship. Grow in your love for all people as Jesus commanded. Choose one of the following activities to do as a family, or design a similar activity of your own.

▶ Help your children write and illustrate a storybook about how your family shows respect for other people and thus honors God.

▶ Talk about what your school does to build a just and kind world. You might use a copy of your school newsletter or visit your school Web site as a guide for your discussion.

■ Our Spiritual Journey

Every person has a call to holiness. Every person has the inner longing to be the person who they were created to be— the image and likeness of God. Living the Ten Commandments is the minimum we can do to travel the road to happiness and holiness. This week at mealtime, pray the prayer on page 273 at the end of the meal.

For more ideas on ways your family can live as disciples of Jesus, visit **BeMyDisciples.com**

A Talent for Everyone

The students in the second grade class wanted to do something special for their families. "Let's put on a talent show!" someone said. Some of the children were very excited.

"I'll play the piano," said Alana. "I can play the drums," John quickly added.

"I can read the poem I wrote," Hector added. "I can jump rope!" said Emily. "And Austin can juggle!"

Some of the children were very quiet. "I don't have a good talent," said Kate.

"But Kate," said Mrs. Chu, their teacher, "you always make us laugh. You are so cheerful and bubbly! What a wonderful quality that is."

"But what will we do for the talent show?" several other students asked.

"Maybe we should stop talking about the talent show," said their teacher. "I think we need to focus on something else first. Each of you is different, and each of you is special. You all have good qualities and talents."

Making Connections

Each of us has good qualities and gifts that God has given us. We can help each other discover our good qualities. We can share our gifts with others.

with Language Arts

Read the book *Stellaluna* by Janell Cannon. *Stellaluna* is about a bat that has the special qualities of a bat. Her bird friends are different from her, but they still get along with Stellaluna, and she with them. Pretend you are Stellaluna. Write an entry for your diary telling what you think and feel about what happened in the story.

with Social Studies

Stellaluna does not have to be just like her bird friends in order to get along with them. Think about your friends. Describe how you are the same and how you are different. Write one way you are different. Tell how this talent can help your family or your class.

with Creative Arts

All people are special. They are children of God. People differ from one another in many ways. Write a slogan that tells about the importance of each person. Make a banner with your slogan on it. Hang it in your classroom or in the hallway at school.

Faith Action

Think about a person in your class who is different from you. Write how that person can help you. Write how you can help that person. Give friendship a chance.

_____

_____

_____

Unit 5 **Review**

Name _____

A. **Choose the Best Word**

Fill in the blanks to complete each sentence.
Use the words from the word bank.

Almsgiving	honor	Golden Rule
Ten Commandments	Grace	Great Commandment

1. The _____ is to love God above
all else and to love people as we love ourselves.

2. _____ means sharing something
to give to the poor.

3. The _____ are the laws God
gave us to help us live happy and holy lives.

4. To _____ a person is to show
that person great respect.

5. When we treat others the same way we want them to

treat us, we are following the _____ .

6. _____ is the gift of God sharing his life with us.

B. **Show What You Know**

Match the words in Column A with their meanings in Column B.

Column A

1. justice

2. Cross

3. obedience

4. fortitude

Column B

___ **a.** sign of Jesus' great love for his Father and us

___ **b.** strengthens us to respect people in authority

___ **c.** good habit of being fair and kind

___ **d.** strengthens us to do what is right and good
when it is difficult

C. Connect with Scripture

What was your favorite story about Jesus in this unit?
Draw something that happened in the story.
Tell your class about it.

D. Be a Disciple

1. *What Saint or holy person did you enjoy hearing about in this unit? Write the name here. Tell your class what this person did to follow Jesus.*

_____

_____

2. *What can you do to be a good disciple of Jesus?*

_____

_____

The Kingdom of Heaven

Jesus said to his disciples,

"At the end of the world, God's own Son will judge all the people. He will divide the good people from those who were not good. He will tell the good people, 'Come into my Father's Kingdom. For when I was hungry you fed me. You gave me clothes when I had none. When I was sick you took care of me.'

"The good people were confused. They said, 'When did we do these things for you?'

"God's Son replied, 'When you did these things for those who needed it most, you did it for me. Now enter God's Kingdom.' "

BASED ON MATTHEW 25: 31–40, 46

What I Know

What is something you already know about these faith concepts?

Making Wise Choices

_____

_____

Conscience

_____

_____

The Our Father

_____

_____

Put an **X** *next to the faith words you know. Put a* **?** *next to the faith words you need to learn more about.*

____ mortal sin   ____ sanctifying grace   ____ consequences

____ Heaven   ____ Kingdom of God   ____ hope

What do you know about the proverbs in the Bible?

_____

A Question I Have

What question would you like to ask about
making good choices to live a holy and happy life?

_____

_____

Chapter 21

We Make Choices

? What was a good choice you made recently?

Some of God's people were not following God's ways. Listen to what Joshua, the leader of the people, told them they had to do.

Whom will you choose to serve? My family and I choose to serve the Lord our God.

BASED ON JOSHUA 24:15

? How can a family serve the Lord?

Humility

Humility helps us to recognize that all we are and all we have comes from God. We are humble when we choose to follow God's ways and make them our own.

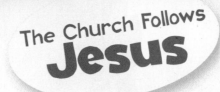

The Church Follows **Jesus**

Saint Francis of Assisi

We have to make choices about the way we want to live. Here is a story about someone who made many important choices.

Francis grew up thinking he would be happy by becoming a rich and famous soldier. So Francis set off to win battles.

But one night, Francis had a dream. In the dream, God asked Francis to return home. Francis chose to do what God asked.

Francis gave away all his riches and began to live a very simple and humble life. Francis chose to serve the Lord.

Today, we know Francis as Saint Francis of Assisi. His followers are called Franciscans. Like Saint Francis, they choose poverty and to humbly serve the Lord. The Church celebrates the feast day of Saint Francis on October 4.

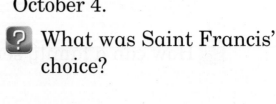 What was Saint Francis' choice?

Saint Francis of Assisi listened to God and chose to do what God asked. Each person has a choice to follow God's Laws. Each person may choose to be a disciple of Jesus.

? What choices have you made when you chose to listen to God?

Activity

Follow the Choices Trail

Read each step along the trail. Circle GR for Golden Rule or the number of one of the Ten Commandments which is being followed as a good choice.

Step 1: I want to watch TV, but I am helping Dad wipe dishes.

4   3   7

Step 2: I want to pretend I'm sick but I go to Mass with my family.

2   3   GR

Step 3: I want to take some gum from the store, because I don't have any money. I wait until tomorrow when I have some money.

7   1   3

Step 4: I want to pinch my sister for making faces at me but I leave the room instead.

GR   10   5

Step 5: I want to copy someone else's homework but I told my teacher I did not understand it.

8   2   7

Faith Words
wise choices
A wise choice is a choice that helps us to live as children of God.

Making Wise Choices

God sent Jesus to show us how to make **wise choices**. A wise choice is one that helps us live as God's children.

Jesus gave us many ways to help us make good choices. Jesus taught us to follow the Ten Commandments. He gave us the Great Commandment. He showed us how to live the Golden Rule.

Jesus always did what his Father asked him to do. We will be truly happy when we make choices as Jesus taught us.

What wise choices do you make to live as Jesus taught us?

God gave us many people to help us make wise decisions. Teachers help us at school, priests help us during the homily at Mass, and parents and families help us at home. God also gave us the Holy Spirit to help us make good choices.

? Who helps you to make wise choices?

Activity

Making Choices

Look and think about what is happening in the pictures. Write what choice you would make next. Share why your choices are wise choices.

_____

_____

_____

_____

_____

Waste not, want not.

Wise Sayings

Wise sayings can help us make wise choices. Think of wise sayings you know, for example, "Buckle Up" or "Stop, Drop, and Roll."

You have learned that the Bible has many wise sayings. They are called proverbs. Proverbs are short, wise sayings that help us to make wise choices. They help us to love God and to follow his commands. They help us choose to live as children of God.

Many of God's people in Old Testament times could not read or write. Listening very carefully and learning proverbs by heart helped them to make wise choices. Wise sayings can help you make good choices too.

? What wise saying helps you to make a wise choice?

Practice makes perfect.

Buckle up for safety!

Remember, the proverbs in the Bible come from God. They helped God's people of long ago make good and wise choices. The proverbs can also help us make good and wise choices today.

Trust in the LORD,
and your plans will succeed.

BASED ON PROVERBS 16:3

❓ What is one of your favorite wise sayings from the Book of Proverbs?

Activity

Choosing Wisely

Draw lines to connect the children to the proverb from the Bible that will best help them choose wisely.

Maireni wonders if she should listen to her mom. Should she plan the best bus route to her friend's house or just go and hope she finds the right way?

Jake wants to be on the basketball team. He wonders, "Should I practice shooting baskets or just play video games?"

Ichiro wakes up, looks out the window, and wonders, "What will this day be like, happy or sad?"

Work hard and become a leader; be lazy and become a loser.

BASED ON PROVERBS 12:24

For the gloomy person, every day is sad; but for the cheerful person, every day is a delight.

BASED ON PROVERBS 15:15

Say no to good advice, and your plans will fail. Say yes to good advice, and your plans will succeed.

BASED ON PROVERBS 15:22

Choose Happiness Forever

God wants us to be happy with him forever. **Heaven** is being happy with God and with all the Saints forever. Making wise choices now will help us find happiness in Heaven.

Praying each day will help us make wise choices. Here is a wise saying about praying from Saint Paul.

Rejoice always. Pray without ceasing. . . . give thanks, for this is the will of God for you in Christ Jesus.

1 THESSALONIANS 5:16–18

Praying every day shows that we are humble and that we know we need God's help to choose wisely. Praying every day shows that we are thankful for all God's gifts to us. Praying every day shows that we want to be happy and that we want to be friends with God today and forever in Heaven.

❓ Why is it so important for us to make wise choices every day?

Remember that Jesus came to show us how to make wise choices. A wise saying in the Book of Proverbs reminds us, "Happy is the person who chooses to make peace" (based on Proverbs 12:20). You choose wisely when you choose to make peace.

I Follow **Jesus**

Activity

My Proverb

Create a wise saying of your own. Help others to see why they should be humble.

_____

_____

_____

_____

_____.

My Faith Choice

This week, I choose to be a peacemaker by speaking kindly. I will remember to

_____

_____.

Pray, "Dear Lord, help me grow in humility. Help me choose to serve you in peace. Amen."

1. It is important for us to make wise choices.

2. Making wise choices now will help us find happiness in Heaven.

3. The proverbs can help us choose wisely.

Chapter Review

Recall

Two words are missing from each sentence. Use words in the box to complete the sentences.

happy	day	wise	proverbs
praying	sayings	Heaven	choices

1. God wants us to be _____ now and forever in _____.

2. Wise _____ can help us make wise _____.

3. _____ from the Bible can help us make _____ choices today.

4. _____ every _____ can help us make wise choices

Reflect

Write the proverb that will help you the most to make wise choices.

_____

_____

_____.

Share What are some of the reasons you will pray this week? Share your reasons with your class.

A Peace Prayer

Saint Francis of Assisi prayed that God would help him to be a peacemaker. Let us pray for God's help to live as peacemakers.

All — **Lord, make us instruments of your peace.**

Group 1 — Where there is hatred,

Group 2 — let us bring love.

All — **Lord, make us instruments of your peace.**

Group 1 — Where there is injury,

Group 2 — let us bring forgiveness.

All — **Lord, make us instruments of your peace.**

Group 1 — Where there is darkness,

Group 2 — let us bring light.

All — **Lord, make us instruments of your peace.**

Group 1 — Where there is sadness,

Group 2 — let us bring joy.

All — **Lord, make us instruments of your peace.**

BASED ON THE PRAYER OF SAINT FRANCIS

With My Family

This Week . . .

In Chapter 21, "We Make Choices," your child learned:

▶ God has created us to be happy now and forever with him in Heaven.

▶ The choices we make can lead us to or away from happiness in this world and the next.

▶ Proverbs are wise sayings in the Bible that help us make wise choices today.

▶ Praying each day will help us make wise choices. It shows that we are humble, needing God's help.

▶ The virtue of humility help us recognize that all our blessings and the blessings of others are from God.

For more about related teachings of the Church, *see the Catechism of the Catholic Church*, 1719–1724 and 2825, and the *United States Catholic Catechism for Adults*, pages 315–317.

■ Sharing God's Word

Read together Proverbs 12:24; 15:15; 15:23; and 16:3, or read the adaptation of these verses on page 287. Emphasize that the proverbs in the Bible can help us make wise choices about how to live as God's children.

■ Living as Disciples

The Christian home and family is a school of discipleship. Choose one of the following activities to do as a family, or design a similar activity of your own.

▶ Choose one of the proverbs in this chapter. Tell how the proverb can help your family live and choose what is right and good. Make it a motto for your family this week. Place it on a card on your refrigerator so that the whole family can see it.

▶ When you make family decisions together, join first in humble prayer. Praying together before decision-making not only strengthens family ties but also helps your children grow in humility as they model the humility you show in seeking God's help through prayer.

■ Our Spiritual Journey

Our spiritual journey finds its end in Heaven. Throughout his ministry, Jesus was continually calling us to Heaven, Pray the prayer of Saint Francis on page 291 this week. Your prayer may make all the difference in this world . . . and in the next.

For more ideas on ways your family can live as disciples of Jesus, visit **BeMyDisciples.com**

Chapter 22

We Can Choose Right from Wrong

? How do we know if a choice is right or wrong?

God wants you to choose for yourself. God also wants you to choose wisely. Listen to what God says in the Bible.

> God lets us choose right or wrong, life or death. Choose what is right. Choose life so that you can be happy with God forever.
>
> BASED ON DEUTERONOMY 30:19

? Why is it important to do what is right?

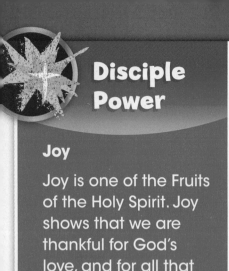

Joy

Joy is one of the Fruits of the Holy Spirit. Joy shows that we are thankful for God's love, and for all that God has made. Joy shows that we enjoy life and delight in making others joyful.

The Church Follows **Jesus**

Paula's Choice

Sometimes, the choices we make are simple ones. But even the simplest choice, if it is a wise choice, can make a big difference. It can bring happiness to us and to others.

When Paula Frassinetti was nine years old, her mother died. Who would take care of her younger brothers? Paula decided that she would.

Paula's choice meant a lot of work for her. She could not go to school. So her brothers shared with her what they learned in school. Paula chose to be cheerful. She went to Mass every day and prayed while she did her chores.

When Paula grew up, she opened a school for poor girls. She later started a religious order to educate children who are poor.

The Church honors her today as Saint Paula. Her feast day is June 11.

❓ Which choices did Saint Paula make? Did her choices make anyone happy? Who?

Activity

Choosing Happiness

Read each statement and think about your day. Circle the happy and sad faces to help you review the choices you have made today.

🙂 🙁 I prayed to God to ask for help.

🙂 🙁 I showed my love to family members.

🙂 🙁 I showed my love to my friends.

🙂 🙁 I showed respect and honor to my teachers and principal at school.

🙂 🙁 I showed my respect to my classmates.

🙂 🙁 I showed my love to other people.

Write one way you will show your love tommorow.

_____

_____

_____

_____

_____

Choosing Right from Wrong

God lets us make choices for ourselves. We can choose to love God or not. We can choose to love others or not. In the Bible we read,

> When God created us, he gave us free choice. It is our choice to do or not to do God's will.
>
> BASED ON SIRACH 15:14–15

Things happen when we make choices. These good or bad things are called **consequences**. We are responsible for the consequences of our actions. This means that we accept what happens because of our choices.

If we make a choice against God's Law, we sin. If we sin, we have to make up for the harm we do.

❓ What are some consequences to a choice you have made? What did you learn from the consequences?

Activity

Choices Have Consequences

Read these stories. Write what you think Sarah or Angel will do. Then draw what will happen next.

Sarah's Choice

Sarah's little sister Katie is sick. Sarah asks her parents, "May I read Katie a story?" But then a friend asks her to come over to play. What will Sarah do?

Angel's Choice

Angel's friend borrows his bike without asking and dents it. Angel thinks he should teach his friend a lesson. He begins to think that he will break his friend's skateboard. What will Angel do?

Catholics Believe

Examination of Conscience

We examine our consciences to know if the choices we made were wise choices. This helps us to live holy lives. We always examine our consciences to prepare to celebrate the Sacrament of Penance and Reconciliation.

Faith Focus
Why is it important to
follow your conscience
when making choices?

Faith Words
conscience
Conscience is a gift
from God that helps us
to make wise choices.

The Gift of Our Consciences

A wise choice is a choice to live as Jesus taught. God gives us a gift that helps us to make wise choices. This gift is called a **conscience**. Our consciences tell us whether a choice we are about to make, or have made, is a wise choice.

The gift of conscience helps us know what is right and what is wrong. Conscience is like a compass. It points us in the right direction. It shows us the way to goodness. It leads the way to happiness.

Making wise choices is very important. We make good choices when we know right from wrong. We learn right from wrong from our families. We learn from the good example of others. We learn from God's rules of love. We learn from the teaching and example of Jesus and from the teaching of the Church.

When we learn and remember what is right or wrong, we are forming our consciences. Then our consciences can help us make good choices. Making wise choices makes good things happen. Making wise choices makes us happy.

? Where do you learn right from wrong?

Let Your Conscience Be Your Guide

These four steps can help you listen to your conscience and make a wise choice.

1. **Think:** What are the possible choices?

2. **Consider:** What might happen next?

3. **Ask:** What does your conscience tell you is the best choice to make?

4. **Act:** Follow your conscience and make your choice.

Read the sentences below. Follow the steps to a decision of good conscience.

Your friend is angry, makes fun of you, and calls you a name. You feel hurt and upset. What do you do?

1. I will **Think** about possible choices.

_____

_____

2. I will **Consider** what might happen next.

_____

_____

3. I will **Ask** what my conscience tells me to do.

_____

_____

4. I will **Act** and follow my conscience.

_____

_____

Faith-Filled People

Saint Philip Neri

Philip Neri made wise choices. He sold all his possessions and gave away his money. He visited banks, shops, and places where people gathered. Every place he visited, he tried to convince people to serve God in all they did. The Church celebrates the feast day of Saint Philip Neri on May 26.

Forming Our Conscience

The gift of conscience tells us whether a choice we are about to make or a choice we have made is a good choice. A good conscience helps us to know right from wrong.

To form a good conscience, we need to learn what God wants us to do.

- We pray to the Holy Spirit.

- We read and listen to the Bible.

- We learn what the Church teaches.

- We ask our parents, teachers, and other grown-ups to help us.

We also need to check, or examine, our conscience. We need to ask ourselves, "How have I loved God or how have I turned away from God?" "How have I loved other people or how have I not loved other people as Jesus taught?" We need to answer these questions honestly. This helps us form our conscience.

? Why is it important to form a good conscience?

A wise choice is a choice to live as Jesus taught. Your conscience helps you to know right from wrong. Your conscience helps you make wise choices.

Activity

Making Choices

Circle the pictures that show children making a good choice to live as Jesus taught. Write an X on the pictures that show a bad choice. Explain your answer.

My Faith Choice

I can choose to make choices to live with joy as Jesus taught. This week, I will

_____

_____.

Pray, "Holy Spirit, help me listen to my conscience. Let me do what is right and pleasing to you. Amen."

TO HELP YOU REMEMBER

1. We are making wise choices when we choose to live as Jesus taught.

2. Wise choices show we are forming and following our consciences.

3. All of our choices have consequences.

Chapter Review

Recall

Unscramble the words.

1. SCICONENCE _____

2. SEQNOCUENCSE _____

3. MINATIONEXA _____

4. SIBLEPONRES _____

5. HOCICE _____

Reflect

Use some of the words above to write a sentence that describes making a wise choice.

_____

_____

_____

_____

_____

_____

Share   Share your sentence that describes making a wise choice with your class.

Be the Joy of My Heart

Saint Augustine chose to change his life and to follow Jesus. He became a bishop in the Church. His choice brought him great happiness. This is his prayer. Pray it with joy.

O God,

Be the light of my life.

Be the life of my soul.

Be the strength of my mind.

Help me choose what is right.

Keep me always in your love.

Be the joy of my heart.

Amen.

BASED ON A PRAYER OF SAINT AUGUSTINE

With My Family

This Week . . .

In Chapter 22, "We Can Choose Right from Wrong," your child learned:

▶ We are responsible for the choices we make and their consequences.

▶ God has given us the gift of a conscience to help us discern right from wrong.

▶ We have the responsibility to form a good conscience to help us live according to God's will.

▶ A well-formed conscience leads to decisions that bring happiness both here and in Heaven.

▶ The gift of joy urges us to choose what makes for happiness.

For more about related teachings of the Church, see the *Catechism of the Catholic Church*, 1716–1724, 1730–1738, and 1776–1794, and the *United States Catholic Catechism for Adults*, pages 314–315, and 341–369.

■ Sharing God's Word

Read together Sirach 15:14–15 or read the adaptation of these verses on page 296. Emphasize that God created us with a free will and the ability to make our own choices.

■ Living as Disciples

The Christian home and family is a school of discipleship. Choose one of the following activities to do as a family, or design a similar activity of your own.

▶ When you watch a TV show together, point out when characters on the show make good choices and when they make bad choices. If someone makes a bad choice, make suggestions for a good choice.

▶ Talk about the choices family members made during the day and their consequences. Such discussion will get your child started thinking about his or her responsibility for the consequences of his or her choices.

■ Our Spiritual Journey

We learn to exercise our free will by practicing discernment. We do so by calling on the Holy Spirit to lead or give direction regarding the choices we make. Discernment can open the door to a new way of life—to a life of joy in the Spirit. Pray the prayer, "Be the Joy of My Heart" on page 303, Encourage your child to ask for guidance in making decisions. Pray together, "*Loving God, be the joy of my heart.*"

For more ideas on ways your family can live as disciples of Jesus, visit **BeMyDisciples.com**

Chapter 23

We Share in God's Life

❓ Tell about a special gift that you have received. What made this gift so special?

Grace helps us to live holy lives. Listen to what the Bible tells us about grace.

Jesus is the living Word of God. He is God's own Son, full of grace and truth. From Jesus, we receive grace and more grace.

BASED ON JOHN 1:14, 16

❓ Who helps you to live a holy life?

Trust

When we trust people, we know we can rely on them. We can depend on them to help us when we are in need.

The Church Follows **Jesus**

A Caring Ministry

Most people in prison have made decisions that have hurt others and themselves. Still, God gives the gift of grace to them through people who care for them.

Jesus tells us that caring for people like prisoners is the same as caring for him. Jesus said,

[I was] in prison and you visited me.

MATTHEW 25:36

Prison chaplains are trained to care for people in prison. They bring the love of Christ to them. The prisoners know they can trust them.

Sister Natalie Rossi, a Sister of Mercy, works at a women's prison in Pennsylvania. Sister Natalie, and prison chaplains like her, show prisoners that God still loves them. She helps them see that God loves them even though they did wrong.

❓ How do prison chaplains like Sister Natalie help people in prison to be open to God's grace?

We are grace-filled people. These are people who can be trusted. When we trust someone, we know that we can depend on that person.

? What are the ways you can be trusted?

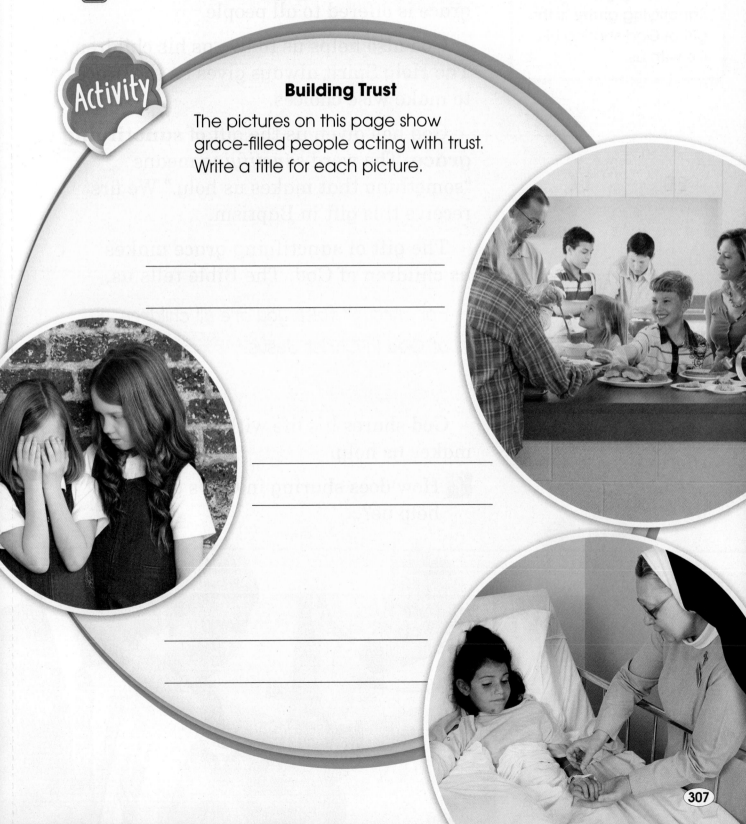

Activity

Building Trust

The pictures on this page show grace-filled people acting with trust. Write a title for each picture.

_____

_____

_____

_____

_____

_____

Amazing Grace

Sister Natalie dedicated her life to sharing God's love with others. She helped others understand that the gift of God's grace is offered to all people.

God also helps us to live as his children. The Holy Spirit always gives us the grace to make wise choices.

God has given us the gift of **sanctifying grace**. The word *sanctifying* means "something that makes us holy." We first receive this gift in Baptism.

The gift of sanctifying grace makes us children of God. The Bible tells us,

For through faith you are all children of God in Christ Jesus.

GALATIANS 3:26

God shares his life with us. God's grace makes us holy.

❓ How does sharing in God's grace help us?

God also helps us to live as his children. The Holy Spirit always gives us the grace to make wise choices. This helps us to live as children of God. Grace helps us live a holy life.

? What is one way you will choose to live a holy life?

Discovering God's Gift

Color the X's one color. Color the O's different colors. Thank God for the wonderful gift of grace.

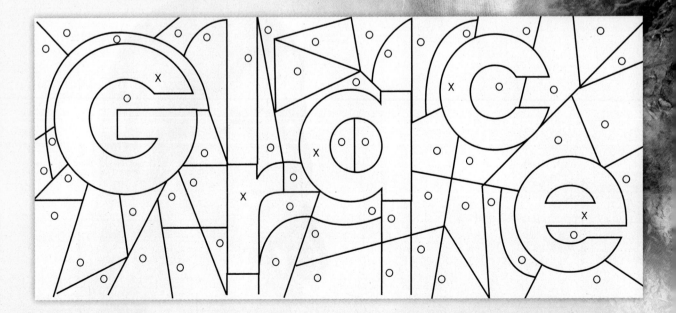

Catholics Believe

The Gift of Peace

Peace is a gift from God through Jesus Christ. Peace is also a fruit or result of the Holy Spirit in us that helps us grow closer to God by the way we care for others in our daily lives.

Faith Words
mortal sin
Mortal sin is a serious sin that causes us to lose the gift of sanctifying grace. We must confess mortal sins in the Sacrament of Penance and Reconciliation.

venial sin
Venial sin is sin less serious than mortal sin. It hurts our relationship with God and other people.

Living a Holy Life

It is not always easy to choose to live a holy life. Sometimes we choose to sin. All sins hurt our relationships with God and other people.

Some sins are very serious. We call this type of sin, **mortal sin**. When we commit serious sins, we lose the gift of sanctifying grace.

We need to confess our mortal sins in the Sacrament of Penance and Reconciliation. When we are sorry for our sins and confess them in the Sacrament, God forgives our sins. We receive the gift of sanctifying grace again. We are filled again with God's life.

? What happens when we sin?

Other sins are not as serious as mortal sins. This type of sin is **venial sin**. It is good to confess these sins too. In the Sacrament of Penance and Reconciliation we receive God's grace to live a holy life. We are at peace.

 What are some of the ways you can show you are truly sorry for your sins?

Activity

Writing a Wise Choice Story

Imagine you are an author. You are writing a book to help people to make wise choices to live a holy life. Write the outline of your story here. Tell your story to a partner and to your family.

Character's name: _____

Wise choice: _____

_____

What happened?

_____

_____

How did the story end?

_____

_____

Jesus Brings Peace

After his Resurrection, Jesus' first word and last gift to his disciples was *peace*.

"Peace be with you," Jesus said to his disciples. "The Father sent me. Now I send you." Then Jesus breathed on them, saying, "Receive the Holy Spirit."

BASED ON JOHN 20:21–22

Peace is Jesus' final, grace-filled gift to us. The gift of peace comes from knowing we are living as friends of God and people.

The Holy Spirit brings us God's peace. The Holy Spirit gives us the help we need to remain in God's grace.

When we are at peace, we are loving God above all else and loving others as we love ourselves. We are living the Great Commandment. We are living the life of grace.

? How does Jesus' gift of peace help us to live the Great Commandment?

God shares the gift of his life with us. Jesus gives us the gift of peace. The Holy Spirit helps us to live as children of God. One way you can live as a child of God is to be a peacemaker. When you show that you can be trusted, you bring peace.

I Follow Jesus

Activity

Signs of Peace

Work with your teacher or parent. Create a message that tells how people your age can live as peacemakers.

_____

_____

_____

_____

_____

_____

My Faith Choice

This week, I will be a person whom others can trust. I will

_____

_____.

Pray, "Thank you, Holy Spirit, for helping me to live as a peacemaker. Amen."

1. Grace is a gift from God.

2. Sanctifying grace is the gift of God's life that he shares with us.

3. The gift of peace helps us live holy and happy lives.

Recall

Match the words to their meanings.

Meanings

a. the gift of God sharing his life with us

b. the choice to say or do what we know is against God's Law

c. the choice that causes us to lose sanctifying grace

Words

___ **1.** mortal sin

___ **2.** sin

___ **3.** sanctifying grace

Reflect

How can we live peaceful and holy lives? Write a sentence to describe one way using words from the chapter.

_____

_____

_____

_____

_____

Share   Share ways you can live as a peacemaker with your class.

Hail Mary

Learn the Hail Mary by heart. Pray it every day to show your love for Mary. Ask Mary to help you bring peace to others.

Leader The Blessed Virgin Mary is full of grace. She was always without sin. She is the greatest and most holy of all the Saints. Let us pray the Hail Mary together and ask Mary to help us to live a holy life.

Group 1 Hail, Mary, full of grace, the Lord is with thee.

Group 2 Blessed art thou among women and blessed is the fruit of thy womb, Jesus.

All **Holy Mary, Mother of God, pray for us sinners, now and at the hour of our death. Amen.**

Leader Now let us raise our voices and ask all the Saints to pray for us.

All **Blessed Saints, please pray for me in your gentle way. Help me learn how I should be. Watch over me each day. Amen.**

With My Family

This Week . . .

In Chapter 23, "We Share in God's Life," your child learned:

▶ God shares divine life with us in the gift of sanctifying grace.

▶ God calls us to live holy lives.

▶ Sin turns us away from God's love and deters us from living holy lives.

▶ Sharing the gift of peace is crucial for living a holy and happy life

▶ When we trust someone, we kow we can depend on them to help us when we are in need.

For more about related teachings of the Church, see the *Catechism of the Catholic Church*, 1846–1869 and 1996–2016, and the *United States Catholic Catechism for Adults*, pages 193, and 328–330.

■ Sharing God's Word

Read together John 1:14, 16. Emphasize that through Jesus we receive the God-given gift of divine help, or grace, to live as children of God.

■ Living as Disciples

The Christian home and family is a school of discipleship. Choose one of the following activities to do as a family, or design a similar activity of your own.

▶ Help your children create peace place mats. Use the place mats at family meals as reminders to share meals in peace and to be peacemakers for one another. Discuss situations where you can show trust.

▶ Point out to your child the many ways your family is "graced." Show your child how to count blessings and so live a holy, happy, and peace-filled life.

■ Our Spiritual Journey

Catholics look upon Mary as the purest of creatures, not subject to the slavery that sin imposes. Catholics believe that Mary is totally graced, totally responsive to the divine will, and totally faithful. God comes to Mary seeking her consent. Mary's "yes" joins the creature to God in the work of completing the labors of creation. Help your child learn the great prayer to Mary, the Hail Mary on page 315. Use it for your family prayer this week.

For more ideas on ways your family can live as disciples of Jesus, visit **BeMyDisciples.com**

Chapter 24

The Our Father

? Who first taught you how to pray? What is your favorite prayer?

Jesus' disciples wanted to know the best way to pray. Jesus taught them:

"This is how you are to pray: Our Father in heaven, hallowed be your name." MATTHEW 6:9

? Do you know the name of the prayer Jesus taught?

Hope

Hope is trusting that God hears us, cares about us, and will always care for us.

A Life of Prayer

The Our Father is the prayer of the whole Church. Catholics all over the world pray the Our Father every day.

Some people in the Church do more than pray every day. They pray all day long. They believe that God has called them to pray always. Convents, abbeys, and monasteries are three of the places where these praying people live. Saint Benedict was one of these praying people.

These people remind us that God is the Father of all people. They trust that God our Father loves us and cares for us. They pray for the Church and for the whole world.

❓ Why is prayer important?

Maybe you cannot pray all day. But you can pray every day. You can pray no matter how you feel. You can make prayer a part of how you live.

? When and how do you pray?

A Prayer Path

Follow the prayer path. At each stop, find a new way to pray and then write your own prayer.

You can share your joy and offer God praise. **I praise you, God, for**

_____.

You can tell God you are sorry. You can ask for forgiveness. **Forgiving God, I am sorry for**

_____.

You can ask God for what you need. You can ask for help for yourself and for others. **Please, God,**

_____.

You can say thanks for the gifts God gives you. **Thank you, God, for**

_____.

Faith Words
Kingdom of God
The Kingdom of God
is also called the
Kingdom of Heaven.
It is a people and
creation living in
friendship with God.

The Our Father

The Our Father helps us to pray to God
and understand how to live as his children.

Our Father, who art in heaven

God is the Father of all people. God creates
us in his image and likeness. God shares his
life and love with us now and forever.

Hallowed be thy name

The word *hallowed* means "very holy."
We love God above all else. We adore and
worship God. We honor and respect the
name of God in all we say and do.

Thy kingdom come

Jesus announced the coming of the
Kingdom of God. The Kingdom of God is
also called the Kingdom of Heaven. When
we love God above all else, we live as Jesus
taught. We prepare for the coming of the
Kingdom of God in its fullness.

? What do you do and say
that show your love for
God the Father?

Understanding the Our Father

Draw lines to connect each part of the
Our Father to its meaning.

Our Father,

who art in heaven,

hallowed be
thy name;

thy kingdom
come,

We say God's holy
name with love.

God's love for us is
now and forever.

The Kingdom of
God is called
Heaven.

God is the Father
of all.

Catholics Believe

Vocation

The word *vocation*
means "what we are
called to do." Every
Christian has the
vocation to live as a
follower of Jesus. God
calls us to do this in
different ways in the
Church.

Faith Words

trespass
To trespass means to do or say something that hurts our friendship with God and with other people.

Thy will be done on earth as it is in heaven

We pray that all will do God's will. The Holy Spirit helps us to continue the work of Jesus. We share God's love with our family, friends, and everyone we meet.

Give us this day our daily bread

We always trust God. God knows what we need. We ask God to help us to live as his children. We pray for all people to receive God's blessings.

And forgive us our trespasses, as we forgive those who trespass against us

Jesus taught us to be forgiving persons. Asking for forgiveness and forgiving others help us to live as children of God and followers of Jesus.

And lead us not into temptation but deliver us from evil

We ask God to help us say no to temptation. Temptation is everything that can lead us away from God's love. The Holy Spirit will help us.

Amen

We end our prayer by saying, "Amen." *Amen* means, "Yes, it is true. We believe!"

What does the Our Father ask us to do?

Understanding the Our Father

Draw lines to connect each part of the Our Father to its meaning.

thy will be done on earth as it is in heaven.

We ask God to help us choose what is good and to protect us.

Give us this day our daily bread,

We believe!

and forgive us our trespasses, as we forgive those who trespass against us;

God gives us what we need.

and lead us not into temptation but deliver us from evil.

We continue the work of Jesus.

Amen.

God forgives us as we forgive others.

The Prayer of All Christians

Christians everywhere pray the Our Father. They pray it in all the languages of the world. Jesus taught that his Father is our Father too. No matter what language we speak, God is our Father.

We love God the Father and trust him. God listens to us. We know he loves us and cares for us.

We also call the Our Father the **Lord's Prayer.** We call it the Lord's Prayer because it is the prayer that Jesus our Lord taught the disciples.

? What does the Lord's Prayer mean to you?

The Holy Spirit is helping you to live the Our Father now. He is helping you to grow in hope. He is helping you to live as a member of the family of God's people.

I Follow Jesus

Activity

A Disciple of Jesus

Put a ✔ next to one way that you could try to live the words of the Our Father this summer. Make a plan to put your choice into action.

____ Pray.

____ Make wise choices.

____ Forgive those who hurt me.

____ Say I am sorry when I hurt someone else.

____ Listen to the Holy Spirit, who helps me to make wise choices.

My Faith Choice

I will live the Our Father. This week, I will do one of the things I checked. I will continue to do the things I checked all summer. I will

_____

 Pray, "Thank you, Holy Spirit, for helping me to live the Our Father. Amen."

1. We pray the Our Father to show our love and adoration of God.

2. The Our Father helps us to live as children of God.

3. The Our Father helps us to prepare for the Kingdom of God.

Chapter Review

Recall

Choose the right word to complete each sentence.

Temptation	**pray**	**Kingdom**
Father	**Hallowed**	

1. _____ means "very holy."

2. When you _____ you lift up your heart to God.

3. God is our _____.

4. _____ is something that leads us away from God.

5. Living as God wants us to live helps us to prepare

   for the _____ of God.

Reflect

What is one way you will choose to live the Our Father?

_____

_____

_____

_____

Share Decorate a paper heart with faith words you learned this year. Now go forth to share your life of faith.

Go Forth!

Jesus taught that we must live our faith in God. Thank God for all you learned this year. Live your faith in Jesus and make a difference. Be his disciple!

Leader We have grown in our faith in many ways this year. Let us thank God!

All **Jesus taught us how to pray.
We can talk to God all day.
Anytime, God always cares.
God always listens,
listens to our prayers.**

Reader 1 Lord, each day we will remember and act like children of God.

All **Thanks be to God.**

Reader 2 Lord, we will love and serve you every day.

All **Thanks be to God.**

Reader 3 Lord, we will treat others with kindness and bring them hope.

All **Thanks be to God.
Jesus taught us how to pray.
We can talk to God all day.
Anytime, God always cares.
God always listens,
listens to our prayers.
Amen.**

With My Family

This Week . . .

In Chapter 24, "The Our Father," your child learned:

▶ Jesus taught his disciples how to pray by teaching them the Our Father.

▶ The Our Father helps us understand how to live as God's children.

▶ When we pray the Our Father, we discover what it means to live as children of God and to prepare for the coming of the Kingdom of God.

▶ The virtue of hope is trusting that God will always act on our behalf.

For more about related teachings of the Church, see the *Catechism of the Catholic Church*, 2777–2856, and the *United States Catholic Catechism for Adults*, pages 481–492.

■ Sharing God's Word

Read together Matthew 6:9–13, where Jesus teaches the Our Father. Emphasize that the Our Father is not only a prayer, it is a "summary of the whole Gospel." Praying the Our Father teaches us how to pray and how to live as children of God.

■ Living as Disciples

The Christian home and family is a school of discipleship. Choose one of the following activities to do as a family, or design a similar activity of your own.

▶ Make an Our Father booklet. As you read each part of the Our Father, write the words of that part in your booklet. Write or draw how you can live each part of the Our Father.

▶ Talk about some of the ways your family lives the Our Father. Pray to the Holy Spirit. Ask the Holy Spirit to help your family live the Our Father each day.

▶ As a family, discuss and list reasons why Christians are a people of hope.

■ Our Spiritual Journey

"**Go in peace**, glorifying the Lord by your life." These words from the Dismissal in the *Roman Missal* send us forth from Mass. They challenge us to live a life worthy of being children of God. Praying the Our Father daily not only reminds us who we are—children of a heavenly Father—but also offers glory to God. Be sure that your children memorize the Our Father. It is part of their Christian identity. Pray it together daily.

For more ideas on ways your family can live as disciples of Jesus, visit **BeMyDisciples.com**

Helping the Community

St. Francis of Assisi parish is having a birthday party! The parish and its school will be twenty-five years old next month.

The second grade class is deciding how it will help plan and celebrate the parish's birthday. The students decide to find out how the parish has helped the community over the last twenty-five years.

The teacher asked the class to interview people in the parish to find ways the parish has helped the community. Each student worked with a partner. Together they decided on who to interview that might remember how the parish has helped others.

The students interviewed family members, older parishioners, the parish priests, and some of the teachers. They discovered that the parish has a lot to celebrate at the birthday party.

The second graders made a big card with a list of all the ways the parish helped the community. Some of the people had given them photographs and they pasted them onto the card. The parish had a very happy birthday party!

WE TAKE PART IN OUR COMMUNITY

We are all important members of the communities where we live. Each of us has a responsibility to contribute to the community.

Making Connections

Every person in a community has a responsibility to take part in the life of that community. This helps others in the community by taking care of one another. St. Francis of Assisi parish helped many people for twenty-five years.

with Social Studies

Saint Francis of Assisi is the patron Saint of St. Francis Parish. The parish wants to remember Saint Francis as part of its celebration by creating a parish Web site about him. Find out something about Saint Francis. Write a paragraph about him and draw a picture with it so it can go on the Web site.

with Language Arts

What do you think were the ways that St. Francis parish helped the community? Find out how your parish or school helps the community. Write a thank you note and send it to the parish pastor or the school principal.

with Creative Arts

Make special Saint Francis of Assisi holy cards. Create a card using a picture of Saint Francis and the Prayer of Saint Francis in this book (Chapter 21, page 290). Share your holy cards with someone special in your life.

Faith Action

Think about one way you can do something for your parish or school. Write it down and pledge that you will do this to help your community. Ask God to help you.

_____

_____

_____.

Unit 6 Review

A. Choose the Best Word

Complete the sentences. Color the circle next to the best choice for each sentence.

1. Our consciences tell us whether a choice we are going to make is a _____ one.

   ○ fun   ○ sad   ○ wise or bad

2. God's gift of sanctifying _____ makes us holy and children of God.

   ○ love   ○ help   ○ grace

3. A very serious sin is called a _____ sin.

   ○ mortal   ○ sanctifying ○ venial

4. Jesus taught his disciples the _____.

   ○ Hail Mary   ○ Our Father   ○ Sign of the Cross

5. The Kingdom of _____. is all people living as God wants them to live.

   ○ Saints   ○ God   ○ Earth

B. Show What You Know

Color the box to mark the sentences that are true.

☐ Proverbs can help us make wise choices.

☐ We are not free to choose to do what is right or what is wrong.

☐ Jesus taught us to pray to God the Father.

☐ Another name for the Our Father is the Jesus Prayer.

C. Connect with Scripture

What was your favorite story about Jesus in this unit?
Draw something that happened in the story.
Tell your class about it.

D. Be a Disciple

1. *What Saint or holy person did you enjoy hearing about in this unit? Write the name here. Tell your class what this person did to follow Jesus.*

_____

_____

2. *What can you do to be a good disciple of Jesus?*

_____

_____

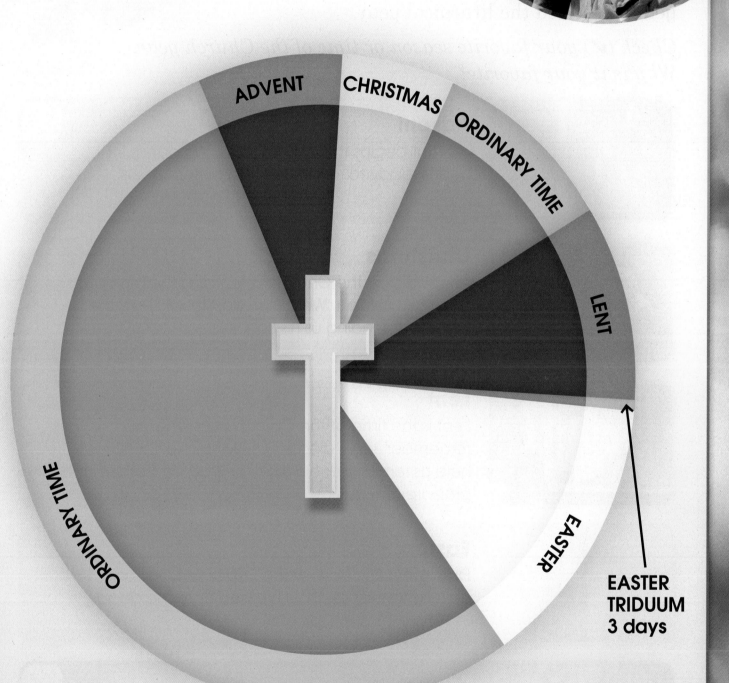

ADVENT

CHRISTMAS

ORDINARY TIME

LENT

ORDINARY TIME

EASTER

EASTER TRIDUUM
3 days

The Liturgical Year

The Church celebrates her faith all year long in prayer and worship The seasons of the Church year are called the liturgical year.

Check (✔) your favorite season or time of the Church year. Why is it your favorite?

Advent

Advent begins the Church year. We get our hearts ready to remember the birth of Jesus.

Christmas

At Christmas, the Church celebrates the birth of Jesus, God's Son. We praise and thank God the Father for sending us his Son, Jesus.

Lent

Lent is the time of the Church year when we remember Jesus died for us. We make sacrifices to help us remember our love for God and others. We prepare for Easter.

Easter

During the fifty days of the Easter season, we celebrate that Jesus was raised from the dead. Jesus gave us the gift of new life.

Ordinary Time

Ordinary Time is the longest time of the Church year. We learn to live as followers of Jesus.

Faith Focus
Why do we honor
the Cross?

**The Word
of the Lord**
This is the Gospel
reading for the
Feast of the
Exaltation of the
Holy Cross. Ask
your family to
read it with you.
Talk about the
reading with
them.

Gospel
John 3:13–17

Exaltation of the Holy Cross

On the Feast of the Exaltation of the Holy Cross, we honor the Cross of Jesus. We remember that, on the Cross, Jesus sacrificed himself for us. We celebrate how, on the Cross, Jesus was the Savior of the entire world.

Saint Paul wrote,

Jesus is God's Son, but he did not act as God. Jesus became man. He became a servant. He loved us and died for us on the cross. That is why God the Father has honored Jesus so highly, blessed his name, and made him Lord of heaven and earth.

BASED ON PHILIPPIANS 2:5–10

The Cross reminds us that Jesus, both God and man, is now Lord of Heaven and Earth. That is why we honor the Cross. That is why the Cross is the great sign of who we are as followers of Jesus.

The Cross of New Life

The Cross was once a sign of sin and death. Now it has become a sign of reconciliation and new life. Honor the cross by decorating it with words and signs of new life.

MY FAITH CHOICE

This week, I will honor the Cross. I will

_____

_____.

Pray, "Jesus, by your holy Cross, you give us new life. Help me to honor that life and share it with others. Amen."

Faith Focus
What do the
Saints show us?

**The Word
of the Lord**
This is the Second
Reading for the
Solemnity of
All Saints. Ask
your family to
read it with you.
Talk about the
reading with
them.

Second Reading
1 John 3:1–3

All Saints

Just as there are members of our family who help us make right choices, there are members of our Church family who show us how to follow Jesus. The people are called Saints. Saints are holy people who love God very much. They live in Heaven with Jesus and see the glory of God. Mary, the Mother of Jesus, is the greatest Saint.

The Church honors all the Saints who live with God in Heaven by setting aside a special feast day. We call this the Solemnity of All Saints. It is celebrated on November 1. We go to Mass and thank God for the Saints in Heaven and for their help.

We believe the Saints intercede for us with their prayers. They help us to live holy lives as children of God.

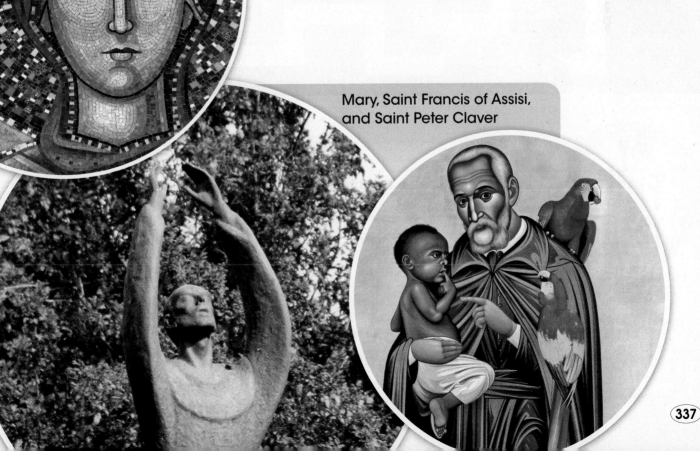

Mary, Saint Francis of Assisi, and Saint Peter Claver

Following Jesus

The Saints show us how to live as followers of Jesus.
Draw yourself next to the Saint below. Draw a line
along the path that will take you to Jesus.

This week, I will live as a faithful follower of Jesus. I will

_____

_____.

**Pray, "Thank you, Lord, for the holy men, women,
and children who teach us to love you. Amen."**

Faith Focus
How does celebrating Advent help us to welcome God into our lives?

The Word of the Lord
These are the Gospel readings for the First Sunday of Advent. Ask your family to read this year's Gospel reading with you. Talk about the reading with them.

Year A
Matthew 24:37–44

Year B
Mark 13:33–37

Year C
Luke 21:25–28, 34–36

What You See
The Advent wreath is made of evergreens. There are three purple candles and one pink candle. The candles stand for the four weeks of Advent.

Advent

Every year, you get excited about your birthday coming. Your family gets ready to celebrate. In Advent, we get ready to celebrate the birth of Jesus. We also celebrate that Jesus is always with us. We celebrate that he will come in glory at the end of the world.

Advent has four Sundays. On these Sundays, we gather in our parish church. Together we get our hearts ready to welcome Jesus. We may sing "O Come, O Come, Emmanuel." *Emmanuel* means "Messiah" or "Savior."

During Advent, we remember that Jesus asks us to do good things. We pray. We try to be extra kind. We help people who need our help.

We Welcome Jesus

Think about ways you can get ready to welcome Jesus.
Write something you can do each day this week.

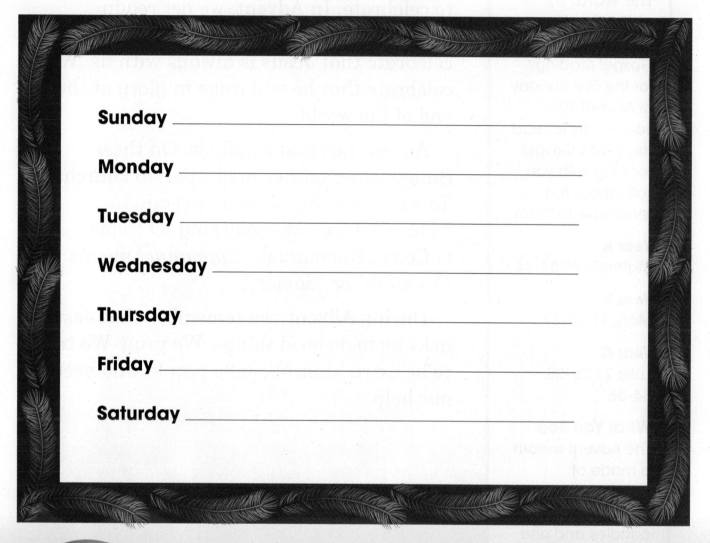

Sunday _____

Monday _____

Tuesday _____

Wednesday _____

Thursday _____

Friday _____

Saturday _____

My Faith Choice

This week, I will prepare for the coming of Jesus. I will

_____

_____.

 Pray, "Oh come, oh come Emmanuel, and save us. Amen."

The Word of the Lord
This is the Gospel reading for the Solemnity of the Immaculate Conception of the Blessed Virgin Mary. Ask your family to read it with you. Talk about the reading with them.

Gospel
Luke 1:26–38

Immaculate Conception

God has a very special love for Mary. The Church has a special love for Mary too. God chose Mary to be the Mother of Jesus, the Son of God. God prepared Mary to be Jesus' mother in a very special way.

God gave Mary a very special grace, or gift. Mary was always free from sin. Mary was born without sin. Mary received God's help all through her life so she would never commit a sin. We call this help from God, "grace."

The angel Gabriel came to Mary to tell her that God had chosen her to be the Mother of his Son. The angel said,

"Hail, favored one! The Lord is with you."

LUKE 1:28

We call this special grace the Immaculate Conception of Mary. We celebrate the Solemnity of the Immaculate Conception of the Blessed Virgin Mary every year on December 8. We honor Mary and her special role as the Mother of Jesus, the Savior of the world.

This day is also a holy day of obligation. This means that Catholics have the responsibility to take part in the celebration of Mass. In this way, we honor God and thank him for the special grace he gave Mary.

Thank You, Mary

In this space, create a thank-you card to Mary.
Write a message. Draw a picture. Thank Mary
for saying yes to God. Thank her for her prayers
and for helping you make good choices.

 **My Faith Choice**

This week, I will honor Mary. I will follow the example
of Mary, the Mother of Jesus. I will

_____

_____

 **Pray, "Mary, God loves you. I love you too. Blessed
are you among all women! Amen."**

The Word of the Lord
This is the Gospel reading for the Feast of Our Lady of Guadalupe. Ask your family to read it with you. Talk about the reading with them.

Gospel
Luke 1:39–48

Our Lady of Guadalupe

Many years ago, Mary appeared to Juan Diego. Juan belonged to the Aztec people who lived in Mexico. Mary asked Juan to go to the bishop of Mexico and ask him to build a shrine. The shrine would be a sign of the love of Mary for all people.

The bishop first asked Mary for a sign. She sent Juan Diego to pick roses from the hill. It was winter, a time when roses did not grow. Juan Diego found the roses. He wrapped them up in his cloak and brought them to the bishop.

When Juan opened his cloak, he and the bishop saw an image of Mary. She was dressed as an Aztec princess. The image of Mary is kept safely in the shrine the bishop built. It is named in her honor as Our Lady of Guadalupe. On December 12, we honor Mary, Our Lady of Guadalupe. We remember her love for all people.

Celebration to the Virgin of Guadalupe, Hilary Simon

Mary, Our Mother

Color the roses in beautiful colors. Under the roses, write one thing you could do to honor Mary.

_____

 **My Faith choice**

This week, I will honor Mary, Our Lady of Guadalupe. I will show my love for all people. I will

_____

_____

 Pray, "Mary, Our Lady of Guadalupe, thank you for your love. Help me love all people as your Son, Jesus, did. Amen."

The Word of the Lord
This is the Gospel reading for Mass on Christmas. Ask your family to read it with you. Talk about the reading with them.

Years A, B, and C
Luke 2:1–14
(Mass at Midnight)

Christmas

Sometimes people tell us good news. Angels told good news to shepherds. They told the shepherds the good news of the birth of Jesus.

The angels praised God for this good news. They sang,

"Glory to God in the highest and on earth peace to those on whom his favor rests."

LUKE 2:14

At Mass, we sing this great song of the angels. We call it the "Gloria." We use their words to sing, "Glory to God in the highest, and on earth peace to people of good will."

345

Give Glory to God

Color in the letters of this prayer. Pray the prayer each day of the Christmas season when you wake up. Pray it again at bedtime.

GLORY to GOD!

This week, I will honor the angels. I will follow their example of telling others about Jesus. I will

_____

_____

 Pray, "Jesus is the Light of the world. Let his light shine everywhere. Amen."

**The Word
of the Lord**
This is the Gospel
reading for the
Solemnity of
Mary, the Holy
Mother of God.
Ask your family to
read the Gospel
reading with
you. Talk about
the reading with
them.
Gospel
Luke 2:16–21

Mary, the Holy Mother of God

Mother's Day is a special day set aside to honor our mothers. We make a special effort to let our mothers know how much we love them. Sometimes we make our moms special cards. We want to thank our moms for loving us.

During the Christmas season, on January 1, we honor Mary. On this day, we celebrate that Mary was blessed by God. She was chosen to be the Mother of Jesus, God's Son. Through the power of the Holy Spirit, the Blessed Virgin Mary became the Mother of Jesus.

We honor Mary, the Mother of God, by going to Mass. We praise God for the gift of Jesus, his Son. We thank God for the gift of Mary, the Mother of God. We ask Mary, our Blessed Mother, to pray for us.

Mary Mosaic. Cartagena de Indias, Colombia

We Thank You, Mary!

Create a Mother's Day card for Mary. Address the card and ask Mary for her help and guidance. Remember to sign your name!

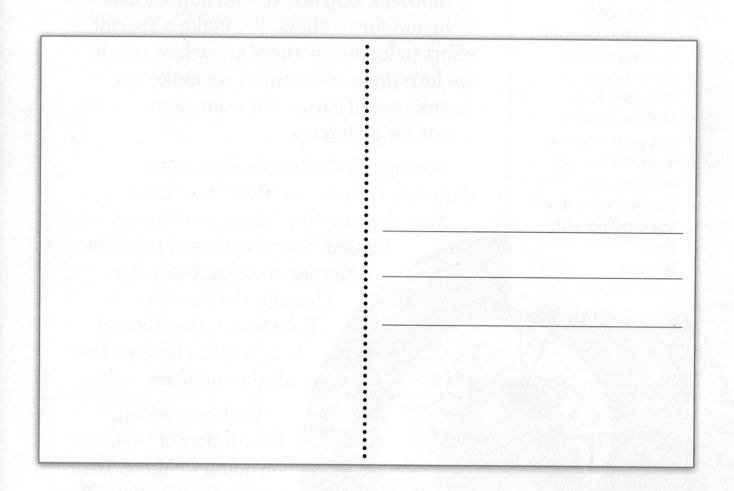

 This week, I will be like Mary, the Mother of God. I will show my love for God by

_____

_____

Pray, "Most loving Mother, Mary, pray for me to the Lord, our God. Amen."

Faith Focus
How did the Magi honor Jesus?

The Word of the Lord
This is the Gospel reading for the Solemnity of the Epiphany of the Lord. Ask your family to read it with you. Talk about the reading with them.

Years A, B, and C
Matthew 2:1–12

Epiphany

We all like to receive gifts. When someone gives us a gift, they are showing us they love us. Long ago, some wise people called Magi gave special gifts to the newborn Jesus.

The Magi saw a bright star in the night sky. They believed that the star was telling them about the birth of a newborn king. The Magi left their homes. They followed the star and traveled many miles to Bethlehem. There they found Jesus with Mary and Joseph. Bowing low, they gave Jesus gifts of gold, frankincense, and myrrh.

The Magi came a long way to honor Jesus. The Gospel story of the Magi reminds us that Jesus welcomes everyone who comes to him.

The Savior of the World

Pretend you are with the Magi on their journey. Follow the maze to Jesus. What gift would you bring to Jesus? What would you say to Jesus when you give your gift to him?

This week, I will follow the example of the Magi. I will

_____

_____

 Pray, "Jesus, King of kings, always guide us to you. Amen."

The Word of the Lord
This is the Gospel reading for Ash Wednesday. Ask your family to read it with you. Talk about the reading with them.

Gospel
Matthew 6:1–6, 16–18

Ash Wednesday

Easter is the celebration of the Resurrection. We celebrate the rising of Jesus from the dead to new life. At Baptism, we receive new life in Jesus too. We share in his Resurrection.

During Lent, we prepare our hearts and minds to celebrate Easter. We remember our Baptism. We make choices to live our Baptism better. Ash Wednesday is the first day of Lent.

We prepare for Easter during Lent by fasting, praying, and doing good things for others. When we go to church on Ash Wednesday, we pray, "A clean heart create for me, O God." We ask God to help us make good choices to live our Baptism. We pray so our hearts will be ready for Jesus.

On Ash Wednesday, the Sign of the Cross is made with ashes on our foreheads. Catholics all over the world wear this cross to show they love God and want to live their Baptism. They want to live as good and faithful disciples of Jesus.

Prayer for Forgiveness

In the Act of Contrition, we tell God we are sorry for our sins. Praying this prayer is one way we can ask for God's forgiveness.

Fill in the blanks to complete the prayer.

My God,

I am sorry for my _____

with all my heart.

In choosing to do _____

and failing to do _____,

I have sinned against you

whom I should _____ above all things.

I firmly intend, with your help,

to do _____,

to sin no more,

and to avoid whatever leads me to sin.

Our Savior Jesus Christ

_____ and _____ for us.

In his name, my God, have mercy.

This week, I will try to memorize the Act of Contrition and ask my family for help. Circle the time you will pray.

† Every morning
† Every afternoon
† Every evening

Pray, "Help me during Lent, Lord, to become more like Jesus. Amen."

Faith Focus
How does celebrating Lent help us to get ready for Easter?

The Word of the Lord
These are Gospel readings for the First Sunday of Lent. Ask your family to read this year's Gospel reading with you. Talk about the reading with them.

Year A
Matthew 4:1–11

Year B
Mark 1:12–15

Year C
Luke 4:1–13

What You See
During Lent the Church uses the color purple or violet. The colors purple and violet remind us of sorrow and penance.

Lent

Sometimes a special day seems far away. But we can do many things to get ready for that day.

During Lent, we do many things to get ready to celebrate Easter. Lent is forty days long. It begins on Ash Wednesday. During Lent, we turn to God and pray each day. We make sacrifices by giving up some things. This helps us to show our love for God and others.

Lent is the special time of the year the Church prepares new members for Baptism. It is the time members of the Church prepare to renew the promises we made at Baptism.

We do all these things during Lent to help us to prepare for Easter. Easter is a special day for all Christians. It is the day of Jesus' Resurrection.

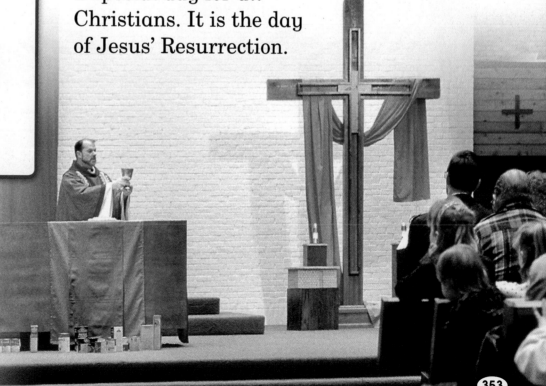

Prepare for Easter

Pick a partner. Take turns answering each question.
Decide how to keep Lent and prepare for Easter.
On the lines, write your answers to each question.

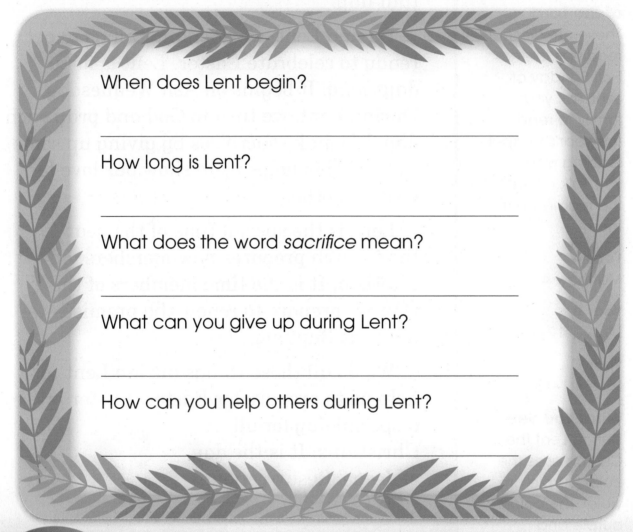

When does Lent begin?

_____

How long is Lent?

_____

What does the word *sacrifice* mean?

_____

What can you give up during Lent?

_____

How can you help others during Lent?

_____

This Lent, I will prepare for Easter. I will

_____

_____.

 Pray, "Jesus, help me to show my love for God and others. Amen."

**The Word
of the Lord**
These are the
Gospel readings
for Palm Sunday
of the Passion of
the Lord. Ask your
family to read
this year's Gospel
reading with
you. Talk about
the reading
with them.

Year A
Matthew
26:14–27:66
or Matthew
27:11–54

Year B
Mark 14:1–15:47
or Mark 15:1–39

Year C
Luke 22:14–23:56
or Luke 23:1–49

What You See
We carry palm
branches in
procession. We
hold them as
we listen to the
Gospel reading.

Palm Sunday of the Passion of the Lord

When friends come to visit, we welcome them. Once when Jesus came to visit Jerusalem, many people came out to welcome him. They spread cloaks and branches on the road to honor him. The Church remembers and celebrates that special time on Palm Sunday of the Passion of the Lord. It is the first day of Holy Week. Holy Week is the week leading up to Easter.

At Mass on Palm Sunday, we honor Jesus. We hold palm branches and say, "Hosanna to the Son of David. Blessed is he who comes in the name of the Lord!" We welcome Jesus as the people welcomed him to Jerusalem.

We Honor Jesus

People sometimes carry banners in processions. Sometimes we hang banners in our church. Banners in our church help us to remember the liturgical season or feast we are celebrating. Decorate this banner.

"Blessed is he who comes in the name of the Lord!"

My Faith Choice

This Holy Week, I will welcome Jesus. I will

_____

_____

Pray, "Blessed are you, Lord Jesus. Hosanna! Amen."

Faith Focus
How does celebrating Holy Thursday help us to grow as followers of Jesus Christ?

The Word of the Lord
These are the Scripture readings for the Mass of the Lord's Supper on Holy Thursday. Ask your family to read one of the readings with you. Talk about the reading with them.

First Reading
Exodus 12:1–8, 11–14

Second Reading
1 Corinthians 11:23–26

Gospel
John 13:1–15

What You See
The priest washes the feet of members of the parish. This reminds us that we are to help others as Jesus taught us.

Many things happen at a family meal. We prepare and cook food. We set the table. We clean up. When we do all these things, we are serving one another.

On Holy Thursday evening, we remember how Jesus showed his love by serving his disciples. Before Jesus and his disciples ate the meal at the Last Supper, he washed their feet. After he finished, he told them to serve others as he served them.

On Holy Thursday evening, we remember all Jesus did at the Last Supper. We especially remember that Jesus gave us the Eucharist.

Prayer for Holy Thursday

The hymn "Where Charity and Love Are Found" is sung in many churches on Holy Thursday evening. The words of this hymn remind us that God is love. We are to love one another as Jesus loved us. Pray this prayer with your class.

Child 1 The love of Christ gathers us.

All **Where charity and love are found, there is God.**

Child 2 Let us be glad and rejoice in him.

All **Where charity . . .**

Child 3 Let us love each other deep in our hearts.

All **Where charity . . .**

Child 4 Let all people live in peace.

All **Where charity . . .**

For this day, I will serve, like Jesus served. I will

_____

_____

Pray, "Lord Jesus, help me to serve others as you did. Amen."

Sometimes something happens to us that brings us suffering. We call this a cross. On Good Friday, we remember that Jesus died on the Cross. We listen to the story of his Passion and Death. We pray for everyone in the world.

On Good Friday, we honor the Cross by kissing it or by genuflecting or bowing deeply in front of it. Our celebration of Jesus' Passion and Death ends with Holy Communion. We walk in procession to the altar and share in the Eucharist. We receive the Body of Christ.

At home we think about how Jesus suffered and died on this day. Our prayers help us to get ready for the joy of Jesus' new life at Easter.

Prayers for the Whole World

On Good Friday, the Church prays a special Prayer of the Faithful. Pray this prayer of the faithful together.

Child 1   May God guide our Church and gather us in peace.

All   **Amen.**

Child 2   May God help the Pope to lead us as God's holy people.

All   **Amen.**

Child 3   May God help those who will soon be baptized to follow Jesus.

All   **Amen.**

Child 4   May God bless our government leaders and help them keep us safe and free.

All   **Amen.**

Child 5   May God fill those in need with faith and hope.

All   **Amen.**

BASED ON THE SOLEMN INTERCESSIONS,
THE PASSION OF THE LORD, *ROMAN MISSAL*

My Faith Choice

On this day, I will honor the Cross. I will

_____

_____.

Pray, "We adore you, O Christ, and we bless you. Amen."

Triduum/Easter Sunday

Faith Focus

Why is Easter the most important season of the Church year?

The Word of the Lord

These are the Gospel readings for Easter Sunday. Ask your family to read the Gospel reading for this year with you. Talk about it with them.

Year A
John 20:1–9
or Matthew 28:1–10
or Luke 24:13–35

Year B
John 20:1–9
or Mark 16:1–7
or Luke 24:13–35

Year C
John 20:1–9
or Luke 24:1–12
or Luke 24:13–35

What is the best day of your life? Why do you say it is the best day you remember? For Christians, Easter is the best day of all days. On this day, God raised Jesus from the dead.

During Easter, we remember that we are one with Jesus Christ, who is risen. For Christians, every Sunday is a little Easter. Sunday is the Lord's Day. It is the day on which Jesus was raised from death to new life.

Easter and every Sunday are days of joy and celebration. On these days, we remember that through Baptism, we share in Christ's new life now and forever.

Celebrating Our New Life

The Earth is filled with signs that remind us of the gift of new life in Christ we receive in Baptism. Find and color the signs of new life in this drawing. Talk with your family about what the signs you discover tell about Easter.

On this day, I will honor the resurrected Christ. I will rejoice in his new life. I will

_____

_____

 Pray, "Christ is risen! Alleluia! Amen."

Faith Focus
What is the
Ascension?

**The Word
of the Lord**
This is the Gospel
for the Solemnity
of the Ascension
of the Lord. Ask
your family to find
the reading in the
Bible. Read and talk
about it with them.

Gospel
Luke 24:46–53

The Ascension of the Lord

After Jesus rose from the dead, he continued to teach his Apostles. He reminded them that soon he would leave them to be with his Father in Heaven. Jesus promised the Apostles that he would send the Holy Spirit to them.

Forty days after Easter, Jesus and the Apostles were in the countryside. He told them that the Holy Spirit would help them to share his teachings with people all over the world.

> [Jesus] raised his hands, and blessed them. As he blessed them he parted from them and was taken up to heaven. They did him homage and then returned to Jerusalem with great joy, and they were continually in the temple praising God.
>
> LUKE 24:50–53

The Church celebrates Jesus' return to his Father in Heaven on the Solemnity of the Ascension of the Lord, forty days after Easter. Jesus promised to prepare a place for us in Heaven. We rejoice that one day we too will share in the glory of Heaven with Jesus and all the Saints.

An Ascension Prayer

*When Jesus rose from the dead and returned
to his Father, he showed us the way to Heaven.
We rejoice in the Resurrection and the Ascension.*

Child 1   Jesus, you rose from the dead.

All   **We celebrate your new life. Alleluia!**

Child 2   Jesus, you promised to send the Holy Spirit.

All   **You are with us always. Alleluia!**

Child 3   Jesus, you ascended to your Father in Heaven.

All   **You will come again in glory to bring us
to our heavenly home. Alleluia!**

My Faith choice

I can prepare for everlasting life in Heaven by living as a
disciple of Jesus. I will

_____

_____

**Pray, "Jesus, show us the way to Heaven. Alleluia!
Amen."**

Faith Focus
Who helps us to live as followers of Jesus?

The Word of the Lord
These are the Scripture readings for Pentecost Sunday. Ask your family to read one of the readings with you. Talk about the reading with them.

First Reading
Acts 2:1–11

Second Reading
1 Corinthians 12:3–7, 12–13

Gospel
John 20:19–23

Pentecost Sunday

What do you do when you have to do something that is very difficult? How do you feel when someone helps you?

Jesus knew it would not be easy for his disciples to do the work he gave them. So he promised that the Holy Spirit would come and help them.

On the day of Pentecost, the Holy Spirit came to Peter the Apostle and the other disciples as Jesus promised. Peter was filled with courage. He told a crowd from many different countries that God had raised Jesus to new life. Everyone was amazed by what Peter was saying. Over 3,000 people became followers of Jesus that day.

The Holy Spirit is our Helper and Teacher too. The Holy Spirit helps us to tell others about Jesus and teaches us to live as followers of Jesus.

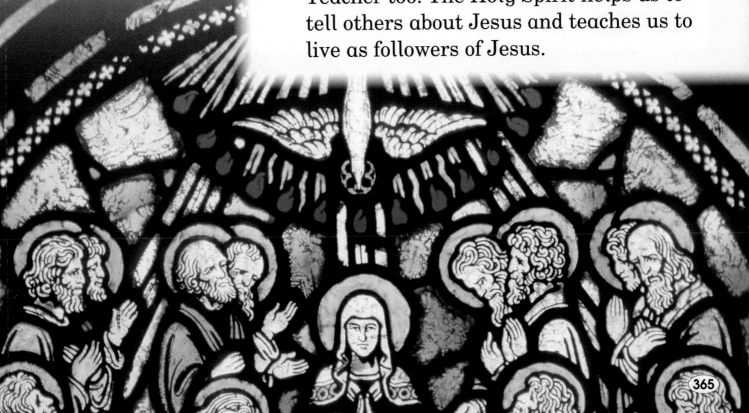

Come, Holy Spirit

The Holy Spirit helps us to live as followers of Jesus. Unscramble the scrambled words in each sentence of this prayer. Write the missing letters of the words on the lines under each sentence. Pray the prayer to the Holy Spirit together.

All — **Come, Holy Spirit, be our guest, in our work,**

be our (ster).   r _____ _____ t

Group 1 — When we are hurt, (lhea) us.   h _____ _____ l

Group 2 — When we are weak, make us (torsng).

_____ _____ _____ **ong**

Group 1 — When we fail, (whas) our sins away.   w _____ s _____

Group 2 — Bring us (jyo) that never ends.   _____ _____ y

All — **Amen.**

My Faith Choice

Like the disciples, I will tell others about Jesus with the help of the Holy Spirit. I will

_____

_____.

Pray, "Come, Holy Spirit, come! Guide us to God! Amen."

Catholic Prayers and Practices

Sign of the Cross

In the name of the Father,
and of the Son,
and of the Holy Spirit. Amen.

Our Father

Our Father, who art in heaven,
hallowed be thy name;
thy kingdom come,
thy will be done
on earth as it is in heaven.
Give us this day our daily bread,
and forgive us our trespasses,
as we forgive those who trespass
   against us;
and lead us not into temptation,
   but deliver us from evil.
Amen.

Glory Be (Doxology)

Glory be to the Father
and to the Son
and to the Holy Spirit,
as it was in the beginning
is now, and ever shall be
world without end. Amen.

The Hail Mary

Hail, Mary, full of grace,
the Lord is with thee.
Blessed art thou among women
and blessed is the fruit of thy
   womb, Jesus.
Holy Mary, Mother of God,
pray for us sinners,
now and at the hour of our death.
Amen.

Signum Crucis

In nómine Patris,
et Fílii,
et Spíritus Sancti. Amen.

Pater Noster

Pater noster, qui es in cælis:
sanctificétur nomen tuum;
advéniat regnum tuum;
fiat volúntas tua,
   sicut in cælo, et in terra.
Panem nostrum cotidiánum
   da nobis hódie;
et dimítte nobis débita nostra,
sicut et no dimíttimus debitóribus
   nostris;
et ne nos indúcas in tentatiónem;
sed líbera nos a malo. Amen.

Gloria Patri

Glória Patri
et Fílio
et Spirítui Sancto.
Sicut erat in princípio,
et nunc et semper
et in sæcula sæculórum. Amen.

Ave, Maria

Ave, María, grátia plena,
Dóminus tecum.
Benedícta tu in muliéribus,
et benedíctus fructus ventris tui,
   Iesus.
Sancta María, Mater Dei,
ora pro nobis peccatóribus,
nunc et in hora mortis nostræ.
Amen.

Nicene Creed

(From the *Roman Missal*)

I believe in one God,
the Father almighty,
maker of heaven and earth,
of all things visible and invisible.

I believe in one Lord Jesus Christ,
the Only Begotten Son of God,
born of the Father before all ages.

God from God, Light from Light,
true God from true God,
begotten, not made,
    consubstantial with the Father;
through him all things were made.
For us men and for our salvation
he came down from heaven,

*(At the words that follow up to and
including* and became man, *all bow.)*

and by the Holy Spirit
    was incarnate of the Virgin Mary,
and became man.

For our sake he was crucified under
    Pontius Pilate,
he suffered death and was buried,
and rose again on the third day
in accordance with the Scriptures.
He ascended into heaven
and is seated at the right hand of
    the Father.
He will come again in glory
to judge the living and the dead
and his kingdom will have no end.

I believe in the Holy Spirit, the Lord,
    the giver of life,
who proceeds from the Father and
    the Son,
who with the Father and the Son is
    adored and glorified,
who has spoken through the prophets.

I believe in one, holy, catholic and
    apostolic Church.
I confess one Baptism
    for the forgiveness of sins
and I look forward to the
    resurrection of the dead
and the life of the world to come. Amen.

Apostles' Creed

(From the *Roman Missal*)

I believe in God,
the Father almighty,
Creator of heaven and earth,
and in Jesus Christ, his only Son,
    our Lord,

*(At the words that follow, up to and
including* the Virgin Mary, *all bow.)*

who was conceived by the Holy Spirit,
born of the Virgin Mary,
suffered under Pontius Pilate,
was crucified, died and was buried;
he descended into hell;
on the third day he rose again from
    the dead;
he ascended into heaven,
and is seated at the right hand of
    God the Father almighty;
from there he will come to judge the
    living and the dead.

I believe in the Holy Spirit,
the holy catholic Church,
the communion of saints,
the forgiveness of sins,
the resurrection of the body,
and life everlasting. Amen.

Morning Prayer

Dear God,
as I begin this day,
keep me in your love and care.
Help me to live as your child today.
Bless me, my family, and my friends
    in all we do.
Keep us all close to you. Amen.

Grace Before Meals

Bless us, O Lord,
and these thy gifts,
which we are about to receive
from thy bounty,
through Christ our Lord.
Amen.

A Vocation Prayer

God, I know you will call me
for special work in my life.
Help me follow Jesus each day
and be ready to answer your call.
Amen.

Evening Prayer

Dear God,
I thank you for today.
Keep me safe throughout the night.
Thank you for all the good I did today.
I am sorry for what I have chosen
    to do wrong.
Bless my family and friends. Amen.

Grace After Meals

We give thee thanks,
for all thy benefits, almighty God,
who lives and reigns forever. Amen.

Act of Contrition

My God,
I am sorry for my sins
    with all my heart.
In choosing to do wrong
and failing to do good,
I have sinned against you
whom I should love above all things.
I firmly intend, with your help,
to do penance,
to sin no more,
and to avoid whatever leads me
    to sin.
Our Savior Jesus Christ
suffered and died for us.
In his name, my God, have mercy.
Amen.

The Rosary

Catholics pray the Rosary to honor Mary and remember the important events in the lives of Jesus and Mary. There are twenty mysteries of the Rosary. Follow the steps from 1 to 5.

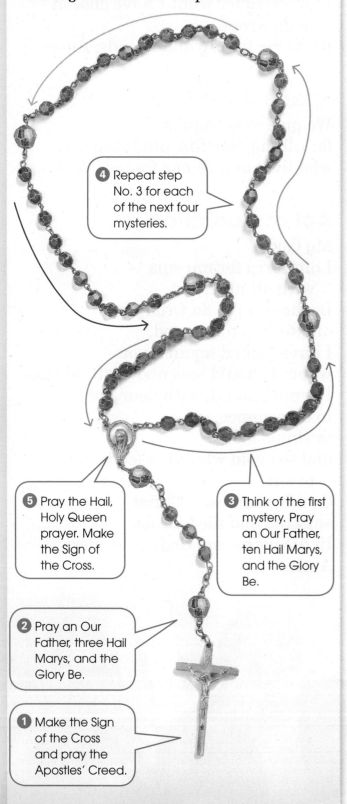

4 Repeat step No. 3 for each of the next four mysteries.

5 Pray the Hail, Holy Queen prayer. Make the Sign of the Cross.

3 Think of the first mystery. Pray an Our Father, ten Hail Marys, and the Glory Be.

2 Pray an Our Father, three Hail Marys, and the Glory Be.

1 Make the Sign of the Cross and pray the Apostles' Creed.

Joyful Mysteries

1. The Annunciation
2. The Visitation
3. The Nativity
4. The Presentation in the Temple
5. The Finding of the Child Jesus After Three Days in the Temple

Luminous Mysteries

1. The Baptism at the Jordan
2. The Miracle at Cana
3. The Proclamation of the Kingdom and the Call to Conversion
4. The Transfiguration
5. The Institution of the Eucharist

Sorrowful Mysteries

1. The Agony in the Garden
2. The Scourging at the Pillar
3. The Crowning with Thorns
4. The Carrying of the Cross
5. The Crucifixion and Death

Glorious Mysteries

1. The Resurrection
2. The Ascension
3. The Descent of the Holy Spirit at Pentecost
4. The Assumption of Mary
5. The Crowning of the Blessed Virgin as Queen of Heaven and Earth

Hail, Holy Queen

Hail, holy Queen, Mother of mercy:
Hail, our life, our sweetness,
    and our hope.
To you do we cry, poor banished children
    of Eve.
To you do we send up our sighs,
mourning and weeping
    in this valley of tears.
Turn then, most gracious advocate,
your eyes of mercy toward us;
and after this our exile
show unto us the blessed fruit
    of your womb, Jesus.
O clement, O loving, O sweet
    Virgin Mary.

The Ten Commandments

1. I am the LORD your God: you shall not have strange gods before me.
2. You shall not take the name of the LORD your God in vain.
3. Remember to keep holy the LORD's Day.
4. Honor your father and your mother.
5. You shall not kill.
6. You shall not commit adultery.
7. You shall not steal.
8. You shall not lie.
9. You shall not covet your neighbor's wife.
10. You shall not covet your neighbor's goods.

BASED ON EXODUS 20:2–3, 7–17

Precepts of the Church

1. Participate in Mass on Sundays and holy days of obligation, and rest from unnecessary work.
2. Confess sins at least once a year.
3. Receive Holy Communion at least during the Easter season.
4. Observe the prescribed days of fasting and abstinence.
5. Provide for the material needs of the Church, according to one's abilities.

The Great Commandment

"You shall love the Lord, your God, with all your heart, with all your soul, and with all your mind. . . . You shall love your neighbor as yourself."

MATTHEW 22:37, 39

The Law of Love

"This is my commandment: love one another as I love you."

JOHN 15:12

The Seven Sacraments

Jesus gave the Church the Seven Sacraments. The Seven Sacraments are signs of God's love for us. When we celebrate the Sacraments, Jesus is really present with us. We share in the life of the Holy Trinity.

Baptism

We are joined to Christ. We become members of the Body of Christ, the Church.

Confirmation

The Holy Spirit strengthens us to live as children of God.

Eucharist

We receive the Body and Blood of Jesus.

Penance and Reconciliation

We receive God's gift of forgiveness and peace.

Anointing of the Sick

We receive God's healing strength when we are sick or dying, or weak because of old age.

Holy Orders

A baptized man is ordained to serve the Church as a bishop, priest, or deacon.

Matrimony

A baptized man and a baptized woman make a lifelong promise to love and respect each other as husband and wife. They promise to accept the gift of children from God.

We Celebrate the Mass

The Introductory Rites

We remember that we are the community of the Church. We prepare to listen to the Word of God and to celebrate the Eucharist.

The Entrance

We stand as the priest, deacon, and other ministers enter the assembly. We sing a gathering song. The priest and deacon kiss the altar. The priest then goes to the chair where he presides over the celebration.

Sign of the Cross and Greeting

The priest leads us in praying the Sign of the Cross. The priest greets us, and we say,

"And with your spirit."

The Penitential Act

We admit our wrongdoings. We bless God for his mercy.

The Gloria

We praise God for all the good that he has done for us.

The Collect

The priest leads us in praying the Collect. We respond,

"Amen."

The Liturgy of the Word
God speaks to us today.
We listen and respond to God's Word.

The First Reading

We sit and listen as the reader reads from the Old Testament or from the Acts of the Apostles. The reader concludes, "The word of the Lord." We respond,

"Thanks be to God."

The Responsorial Psalm

The song leader leads us in singing a psalm.

The Second Reading

The reader reads from the New Testament, but not from the four Gospels. The reader concludes, "The word of the Lord." We respond,

"Thanks be to God."

The Acclamation

We stand to honor Christ, present with us in the Gospel. The song leader leads us in singing **"Alleluia, Alleluia, Alleluia,"** or another chant during Lent.

The Gospel

The deacon or priest proclaims, "A reading from the holy Gospel according to (name of Gospel writer)." We respond,

"Glory to you, O Lord."

He proclaims the Gospel. At the end he says, "The Gospel of the Lord." We respond,

"Praise to you, Lord Jesus Christ."

The Homily

We sit. The priest or deacon preaches the Homily. He helps the people gathered to understand the Word of God spoken to us in the readings.

The Profession of Faith

We stand and profess our faith. We pray the Nicene Creed together.

The Prayer of the Faithful

The priest leads us in praying for our Church and her leaders, for our country and its leaders, for ourselves and others, for those who are sick and those who have died. We can respond to each prayer in several ways. One way that we respond is,

"Lord, hear our prayer."

The Liturgy of the Eucharist

We join with Jesus and the Holy Spirit
to give thanks and praise to God the Father.

The Preparation of the Altar and Gifts

We sit as the altar is prepared and the collection is taken up. We share our blessings with the community of the Church and especially with those in need. The song leader may lead us in singing a song. The gifts of bread and wine are brought to the altar.

The priest lifts up the bread and blesses God for all our gifts. He prays, "Blessed are you, Lord God of all creation. . . ." We respond,

"Blessed be God for ever."

The priest lifts up the chalice of wine and prays, "Blessed are you, Lord God of all creation. . . ."
We respond,

"Blessed be God for ever."

The priest invites us,
"Pray, brethren (brother and sisters), that my sacrifice and yours may be acceptable to God, the almighty Father."

We stand and respond,

"May the Lord accept the sacrifice at your hands for the praise and glory of his name, for our good and the good of all his holy Church."

The Prayer over the Offerings

The priest leads us in praying the Prayer over the Offerings.
We respond, **"Amen."**

Opening Dialogue and Preface

The priest invites us to join in praying the Church's great prayer of praise and thanksgiving to God the Father.

Priest: "The Lord be with you."

Assembly: "And with your spirit."

Priest: "Lift up your hearts."

Assembly: "We lift them up to the Lord."

Priest: "Let us give thanks to the Lord our God."

Assembly: "It is right and just."

After the priest sings or prays aloud the Preface, we join in acclaiming,

**"Holy, Holy, Holy Lord God of hosts.
Heaven and earth are full of your glory.
Hosanna in the highest.
Blessed is he who comes in the name of the Lord.
Hosanna in the highest."**

The Eucharistic Prayer

The priest leads the assembly in praying the Eucharistic Prayer.

We call on the Holy Spirit to make our gifts of bread and wine holy so that they become the Body and Blood of Jesus. We recall what happened at the Last Supper. The bread and wine become the Body and Blood of the Lord. Jesus is truly and really present under the appearances of bread and wine.

The priest sings or says aloud, "The mystery of faith." We respond using this or another acclamation used by the Church,

"We proclaim your Death, O Lord, and profess your Resurrection until you come again."

The priest then prays for the Church. He prays for the living and the dead.

Doxology

The priest concludes the praying of the Eucharistic Prayer. He sings or prays aloud,

**"Through him, and with him, and in him,
O God, almighty Father,
in the unity of the Holy Spirit,
all glory and honor is yours,
for ever and ever."**

We respond by singing, **"Amen."**

The Communion Rite

The Lord's Prayer
We pray the Lord's Prayer together.

The Sign of Peace
The priest invites us to share a sign of peace, saying, "The peace of the Lord be with you always." We respond,
"And with your spirit."
We share a sign of peace.

The Fraction, or the Breaking of the Bread
The priest breaks the host, the consecrated bread. We sing or pray aloud,

**"Lamb of God, you take away the sins of the world,
   have mercy on us.
Lamb of God, you take away the sins of the world,
   have mercy on us.
Lamb of God, you take away the sins of the world,
   grant us peace."**

Communion
The priest raises the host and says aloud,

"Behold the Lamb of God, behold him who takes away the sins of the world.
Blessed are those called to the supper of the Lamb."

We join with him and say,
"Lord, I am not worthy that you should enter under my roof, but only say the word and my soul shall be healed."

The priest receives Communion. Next, the deacon, the extraordinary ministers of Holy Communion, and the members of the assembly receive Communion.

The priest, deacon, or extraordinary minister of Holy Communion holds up the host. We bow, and the priest, deacon, or extraordinary minister of Holy Communion says, "The Body of Christ." We respond, **"Amen."** We then receive the consecrated host in our hands or on our tongues.

If we are to receive the Blood of Christ, the priest, deacon, or extraordinary minister of Holy Communion holds up the cup containing the consecrated wine. We bow, and the priest, deacon, or extraordinary minister of Holy Communion says, "The Blood of Christ." We respond, **"Amen."** We take the cup in our hands and drink from it.

The Prayer After Communion
We stand as the priest invites us to pray, saying, "Let us pray." He prays the Prayer After Communion. We respond, **"Amen."**

The Concluding Rites
We are sent forth to do good works,
praising and blessing the Lord.

Greeting
We stand. The priest greets us as we prepare to leave. He says, "The Lord be with you." We respond, **"And with your spirit."**

Final Blessing
The priest or deacon may invite us,
"Bow down for the blessing."
The priest blesses us, saying,
"May almighty God bless you,
the Father, and the Son,
and the Holy Spirit."
We respond, **"Amen."**

Dismissal of the People
The priest or deacon sends us forth, using these or similar words,
"Go in peace, glorifying the Lord by your life."
We respond,
"Thanks be to God."
We sing a hymn. The priest and the deacon kiss the altar. The priest, deacon, and other ministers bow to the altar and leave in procession.

The Sacrament of Penance and Reconciliation

Individual Rite
Greeting
Scripture Reading
Confession of Sins
   and Acceptance of Penance
Act of Contrition
Absolution
Closing Prayer

Communal Rite
Greeting
Scripture Reading
Homily
Examination of Conscience, a
   Litany of Contrition, and the
   Lord's Prayer
Individual Confession and Absolution
Closing Prayer

A Visit to Church

Catholic churches are built in many styles and sizes. Some Catholic churches are older and some are newer. Some are big and some are small. But, all churches are places where people worship God.

Baptismal Font

As you enter a Catholic church, you may see a baptismal font. The baptismal font is the pool of water used for the Sacrament of Baptism. Water is used to remind us of new life.

Ambo

The ambo is the special place from where the Word of God, the Scriptures, is read. The lector is the person who reads the first and second readings during Mass. The deacon or priest reads the Gospel.

Paschal Candle

During the Easter Season, the Paschal candle, also called the Easter candle, is placed near the baptismal font. It reminds us of Jesus, the Light of the world.

Assembly

The assembly is the people gathered for Mass. The pews are the seats where the people sit.

The Book of the Gospels Lectionary

The Book of the Gospels contains the Gospel readings we listen to at Mass. The first two readings are read from the Lectionary.

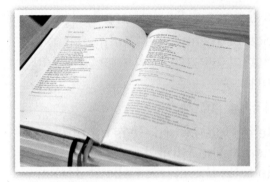

Crucifix

You will see a crucifix or cross that might be carried in procession by one of the servers. Or, it might be a crucifix or cross hanging from the ceiling or hung on the wall.

Tabernacle

The tabernacle is the place in the church where the Eucharist or Blessed Sacrament is kept. Some churches have a chapel where people can pray. When the candle next to the tabernacle is lit, it means that the Blessed Sacrament is in the tabernacle.

Altar

The altar is where the Liturgy of the Eucharist is celebrated at Mass. It reminds us of the Last Supper and that Jesus died for us. It is the table from which Jesus shares his Body and Blood with us.

It is very important to remember that through the Church, Christ continues to be with us in the world. The Church is every one of us, the People of God.

Key Teachings of the Catholic Church

The Mystery of God

Divine Revelation

Who am I?

You are a person created by God. God wants you to live in friendship with him on earth and forever in Heaven.

How do we know this about ourselves?

God knows and loves all people. God wants us to know and love him too. God tells us about ourselves. God also tells us about himself.

How did God tell us?

God tells us in many ways. First, all the things God has created tell us about him. We see God's goodness and beauty in creation. Second, God came to us and told us about himself. He told us the most when he sent his Son, Jesus Christ. God's Son became one of us and lived among us. He showed us who God is.

What is faith?

Faith is a gift from God. It helps us to know and to believe in God.

What is a mystery of faith?

A mystery of faith can never be known completely. We cannot know everything about God. We only know who God is because he told us about himself.

What is Divine Revelation?

God wants us to know about him. Divine Revelation is how he freely makes himself known to us. God has told us about himself and his plan for us. He has done this so that we can live in friendship with him and with one another forever.

What is Sacred Tradition?

The word *tradition* means "to pass on." The Church's Sacred Tradition passes on what God has told us. The Holy Spirit guides the Church to tell us about God.

Sacred Scripture

What is Sacred Scripture?

Sacred Scripture means "holy writings." Sacred Scripture are writings that tell God's story.

What is the Bible?

The Bible is God's word. It is a holy book. The stories in the Bible teach about God. The Bible tells the stories about Jesus. When you listen to the Bible, you are listening to God.

What does it mean to say that the Bible is inspired?

This means that the Holy Spirit helped people write about God. The Holy Spirit helped the writers tell what God wants us to know about him.

What is the Old Testament?

The Old Testament is the first part of the Bible. It has forty-six books. They were written before the birth of Jesus. The Old Testament tells the story of creation. It tells about Adam and Eve. It tells about the promise, or Covenant, between God and his people.

What is the Covenant?

The Covenant is the promise that God and his people freely made. It is God's promise always to love and be kind to his people.

What are the writings of the prophets?

God chose people to speak in his name. These people are called the prophets. We read the message of the prophets in the Bible. The prophets remind God's people that God is faithful. They remind God's people to be faithful to the Covenant.

What is the New Testament?

The New Testament is the second part of the Bible. It has twenty-seven books. These books were inspired by the Holy Spirit. They were written during the time of the Apostles. They are about Jesus Christ. They tell about his saving work.

What are the Gospels?

The Gospels are the four books at the beginning of the New Testament. They tell the story of Jesus and his teachings. The four Gospels are Matthew, Mark, Luke, and John.

What are the letters of Saint Paul?

The letters of Saint Paul are in the New Testament. The letters teach about the Church. They tell how to follow Jesus. Many of these letters were written before the Gospels.

The Holy Trinity

Who is the Mystery of the Holy Trinity?

The Holy Trinity is the mystery of One God in Three Persons—God the Father, God the Son, and God the Holy Spirit.

Who is God the Father?

God the Father is the First Person of the Holy Trinity.

Who is God the Son?

God the Son is Jesus Christ. He is the Second Person of the Holy Trinity. God the Father sent his Son to be one of us and live with us.

Who is God the Holy Spirit?

The Holy Spirit is the Third Person of the Holy Trinity. God sends us the Holy Spirit to help us to know and love God better. The Holy Spirit helps us live as children of God.

Divine Work of Creation

What does it mean to call God the Creator?

God is the Creator. He has made everyone and everything out of love. He has created everyone and everything without any help.

Who are angels?

Angels are spiritual beings. They do not have bodies like we do. Angels give glory to God at all times. They sometimes serve God by bringing his message to people.

Why are human beings special?

God creates every human being in his image and likeness. God shares his life with us. God wants us to be happy with him forever.

What is the soul?

The soul is the spiritual part of a person. The soul will never die. It is the part of us that lives forever. It bears the image of God.

What is free will?

Free will is the power God gives us to choose between good and evil. Free will gives us the power to turn toward God.

What is Original Sin?

Original Sin is the sin of Adam and Eve. They chose to disobey God. As a result of Original Sin, death, sin, and suffering came into the world.

Jesus Christ, Son of God, Son of Mary

What is the Annunciation?

At the Annunciation the angel Gabriel came to Mary. The angel had a message for her. God had chosen her to be the Mother of his Son, Jesus.

What is the Incarnation?

The Incarnation is the Son of God becoming a man and still being God. Jesus Christ is true God and true man.

What does it mean that Jesus is Lord?

The word *lord* means "master or ruler." When we call Jesus "Lord," we mean that he is truly God.

What is the Paschal Mystery?

The Paschal Mystery is the Passion, Death, Resurrection, and Ascension of Jesus Christ. Jesus passed over from death into new and glorious life.

What is Salvation?

The word *salvation* means "to save." It is the saving of all people from sin and death through Jesus Christ.

What is the Resurrection?

The Resurrection is God's raising Jesus from the dead to new life.

What is the Ascension?

The Ascension is the return of the Risen Jesus to his Father in Heaven.

What is the Second Coming of Christ?

Christ will come again in glory at the end of time. This is the Second Coming of Christ. He will judge the living and the dead. This is the fulfillment of God's plan.

What does it mean that Jesus is the Messiah?

The word *messiah* means "anointed one." He is the Messiah. God promised to send the Messiah to save all people. Jesus is the Savior of the world.

The Mystery of the Church

What is the Church?

The word *church* means "those who are called together." The Church is the Body of Christ. It is the new People of God.

What does the Church do?

The Church tells all people the Good News of Jesus Christ. The Church invites all people to know, love, and serve Jesus.

What is the Body of Christ?

The Church is the Body of Christ on Earth. Jesus Christ is the Head of the Church and all baptized people are its members.

Who are the People of God?

The Church is the People of God. God invites all people to belong to the People of God. The People of God live as one family in God.

What is the Communion of Saints?

The Communion of Saints is all of the holy people that make up the Church. It is the faithful followers of Jesus on earth. It is those who have died who are still becoming holier. It is also those who have died and are happy forever with God in Heaven.

What are the Marks of the Church?

There are four main ways to describe the Church. We call these the four Marks of the Church. The Church is one, holy, catholic, and apostolic.

Who are the Apostles?

The Apostles were the disciples whom Jesus chose. He sent them to preach the Gospel to the whole world in his name. Some of their names are Peter, Andrew, James, and John.

What is Pentecost?

Pentecost is the day the Holy Spirit came to the disciples of Jesus. This happened fifty days after the Resurrection. The work of the Church began on this day.

Who are the clergy?

The clergy are bishops, priests, and deacons. They have received the Sacrament of Holy Orders. They serve the whole Church.

What is the work of the Pope?

Jesus Christ is the true Head of the Church. The Pope and the bishops lead the Church in his name. The Pope is the bishop of Rome. He is the successor to Saint Peter the Apostle, the first Pope. The Pope brings the Church together. The Holy Spirit guides the Pope when he speaks about faith, and about what Catholics believe.

What is the work of the bishops?

The other bishops are the successors of the other Apostles. They teach and lead the Church in their dioceses. The Holy Spirit always guides the Pope and all of the bishops. He guides them when they make important decisions.

What is religious life?

Some men and women want to follow Jesus in a special way. They choose the religious life. They promise not to marry. They dedicate their whole lives to doing Jesus' work. They promise to live holy lives. They promise to live simply. They share what they have with others. They live together in groups and they promise to obey the rules of their community. They may lead quiet lives of prayer, or teach, or take care of people who are sick or poor.

Who are laypeople?

Many people do not receive the Sacrament of Holy Orders. Many are not members of a religious community. These are laypeople. Laypeople follow Christ every day by what they do and say.

The Blessed Virgin Mary

Who is Mary?

God chose Mary to be the Mother of his only Son, Jesus. Mary is the Mother of God. She is the Mother of Jesus. She is the Mother of the Church. Mary is the greatest Saint.

What is the Immaculate Conception?

From the first moment of her being, Mary was preserved from sin. This special grace from God continued throughout her whole life. We call this the Immaculate Conception.

What is the Assumption of Mary?

At the end of her life on Earth, the Blessed Virgin Mary was taken body and soul into Heaven. Mary hears our prayers. She tells her Son what we need. She reminds us of the life that we all hope to share when Christ, her Son, comes again in glory.

Life Everlasting

What is eternal life?

Eternal life is life after death. At death the soul leaves the body. It passes into eternal life.

What is Heaven?

Heaven is living with God and with Mary and all the Saints in happiness forever after we die.

What is the Kingdom of God?

The Kingdom of God is also called the Kingdom of Heaven. It is all people and creation living in friendship with God.

What is purgatory?

Purgatory is the chance to grow in love for God after we die so we can live forever in Heaven.

What is hell?

Hell is life away from God and the Saints forever after death.

Celebration of the Christian Life and Mystery

Liturgy and Worship

What is worship?

Worship is the praise we give God. The Church worships God in the liturgy.

What is liturgy?

The liturgy is the Church's worship of God. It is the work of the Body of Christ. Christ is present by the power of the Holy Spirit.

What is the liturgical year?

The liturgical year is the name of the seasons and feasts that make up the Church year of worship. The main seasons of the Church year are Advent, Christmas, Lent, and Easter. The Triduum is the three holy days just before Easter. The rest of the liturgical year is called Ordinary Time.

The Sacraments

What are the Sacraments?

The Sacraments are the seven signs of God's love for us that Jesus gave the Church. We share in God's love when we celebrate the Sacraments.

What are the Sacraments of Christian Initiation?

The Sacraments of Christian Initiation are Baptism, Confirmation, and Eucharist.

What is the Sacrament of Baptism?

Baptism joins us to Christ. It makes us members of the Church. We receive the gift of the Holy Spirit. Original Sin and our personal sins are forgiven. Through Baptism, we belong to Christ.

What is the Sacrament of Confirmation?

At Confirmation, we receive the gift of the Holy Spirit. The Holy Spirit strengthens us to live our Baptism.

What is the Sacrament of Eucharist?

In the Eucharist, we join with Christ. We give thanksgiving, honor, and glory to God the Father. Through the power of the Holy Spirit, the bread and wine become the Body and Blood of Jesus Christ.

Why do we have to participate at Sunday Mass?

Catholics participate in the Eucharist on Sundays and holy days of obligation. Sunday is the Lord's Day. Participating at the Mass and receiving Holy Communion, the Body and Blood of Christ, when we are old enough, are necessary for Catholics.

What is the Mass?

The Mass is the main celebration of the Church. At Mass, we worship God. We listen to God's Word. We celebrate and share in the Eucharist.

What are the Sacraments of Healing?

The two Sacraments of Healing are the Sacrament of Penance and Reconciliation and the Sacrament of the Anointing of the Sick.

What is confession?

Confession is telling our sins to a priest in the Sacrament of Penance and Reconciliation. Confession is another name for the Sacrament.

What is contrition?

Contrition is being truly sorry for our sins. We want to make up for the hurt our sins have caused. We do not want to sin again.

What is penance?

A penance is a prayer or act of kindness. The penance we do shows that we are truly sorry for our sins. The priest gives us a penance to help repair the hurt caused by our sin.

What is absolution?

Absolution is the forgiveness of sins by God through the words and actions of the priest.

What is the Sacrament of the Anointing of the Sick?

The Sacrament of the Anointing of the Sick is one of the two Sacraments of Healing. We receive this Sacrament when we are very sick, old, or dying. This Sacrament helps make our faith and trust in God strong.

What are the Sacraments at the Service of Communion?

Holy Orders and Matrimony, or marriage, are the two Sacraments at the Service of Communion. People who receive these Sacraments serve God.

What is the Sacrament of Holy Orders?

In this Sacrament, baptized men are consecrated as bishops, priests, or deacons. They serve the whole Church. They serve in the name and person of Christ.

Who is a bishop?

A bishop is a priest. He receives the fullness of the Sacrament of Holy Orders. He is a successor to the Apostles. He leads and serves in a diocese. He teaches and leads worship in the name of Jesus.

Who is a priest?

A priest is a baptized man who receives the Sacrament of Holy Orders. Priests work with their bishops. The priest teaches about the Catholic faith. He celebrates Mass. Priests help to guide the Church.

Who is a deacon?

A deacon is ordained to help bishops and priests. He is not a priest. He is ordained to serve the Church.

What is the Sacrament of Matrimony?

In the Sacrament of Matrimony, or marriage, a baptized man and a baptized woman make a lifelong promise. They promise to serve the Church as a married couple. They promise to love each other. They show Christ's love to others.

What are the sacramentals of the Church?

Sacramentals are objects and blessings the Church uses. They help us worship God.

Life in the Spirit

The Moral Life

Why did God create us?

God created us to give honor and glory to him. God created us to live a life of blessing with him here on Earth and forever in Heaven.

What does it mean to live a moral life?

God wants us to be happy. He gives us the gift of his grace. When we accept God's gift by living the way Jesus taught us, we are living a moral life.

What is the Great Commandment?

Jesus taught us to love God above all else. He taught us to love our neighbors as ourselves. This is the path to happiness.

What are the Ten Commandments?

The Ten Commandments are the laws that God gave Moses. They teach us to live as God's people. They teach us to love God, others, and ourselves.

The Commandments are written on the hearts of all people.

What are the Beatitudes?

The Beatitudes are teachings of Jesus. They tell us what real happiness is. The Beatitudes tell us about the Kingdom of God. They help us live as followers of Jesus. They help us keep God at the center of our lives.

What are the Works of Mercy?

God's love and kindness is at work in the world. This is what mercy is. Human works of mercy are acts of loving kindness. We reach out to people. We help them with what they need for their bodies and their spirits.

What are the Precepts of the Church?

The Precepts of the Church are five rules. These rules help us worship God and grow in love of God and our neighbors.

Holiness of Life and Grace

What is holiness?

Holiness is life with God. Holy people are in right relationship with God, with people, and with all of creation.

What is grace?

Grace is the gift of God sharing his life and love with us.

What is sanctifying grace?

Sanctifying grace is the grace we receive at Baptism. It is a free gift of God, given by the Holy Spirit.

What are the Gifts of the Holy Spirit?

The seven Gifts of the Holy Spirit help us to live our Baptism. They are wisdom, understanding, right judgment, courage, knowledge, reverence, and wonder and awe.

The Virtues

What are the virtues?

The virtues are spiritual powers or habits. The virtues help us to do what is good.

What are the most important virtues?

The most important virtues are the three virtues of faith, hope, and love. These virtues are gifts from God. They help us keep God at the center of our lives.

What is conscience?

A conscience. is a gift God gives to every person. It helps us know and judge what is right and what is wrong. Our conscience moves us to do good and avoid evil.

Evil and Sin

What is evil?

Evil is the harm we choose to do to one another and to God's creation.

What is temptation?

Temptations are feelings, people, and things that try to get us to turn away from God's love and not live a holy life.

What is sin?

Sin is freely choosing to do or say something that we know God does not want us to do or say.

What is mortal sin?

A mortal sin is doing or saying something on purpose that is very bad. A mortal sin is against what God wants us to do or say. When we commit a mortal sin, we lose sanctifying grace.

What are venial sins?

Venial sins are sins that are less serious than mortal sins. They weaken our love for God and one another. They make us less holy.

Christian Prayer

What is prayer?

Prayer is talking to and listening to God. When we pray, we raise our minds and hearts to God the Father, Son, and Holy Spirit.

What is the Our Father?

The Lord's Prayer, or Our Father, is the prayer of all Christians. Jesus taught his disciples the Our Father. Jesus gave this prayer to the Church. When we pray the Our Father, we come closer to God and to his Son, Jesus Christ. The Our Father helps us become like Jesus.

What kinds of prayer are there?

Some kinds of prayer use words that we say aloud or quietly in our hearts. Some silent prayers use our imagination to bring us closer to God. Another silent prayer is simply being with God.

Glossary

A

almighty [page 52]

God alone is almighty. This means that only God has the power to do everything good.

Ascension [page 92]

The Ascension is the return of the Risen Jesus to his Father in Heaven forty days after the Resurrection.

assembly [page 176]

The assembly is the People of God gathered to celebrate Mass. All members of the assembly share in the celebration of Mass.

B

Baptism [page 134]

Baptism is the Sacrament that joins us to Christ and makes us members of the Church. We receive the gift of the Holy Spirit and become adopted sons and daughters of God.

believe [page 26]

To believe in God means to know God and to give ourselves to him with all our hearts.

Bible [page 14]

The Bible is the written Word of God.

Body of Christ [page 106]

The Church is the Body of Christ. Jesus Christ is the Head of the Church. All the baptized are members of the Church.

C

Communion of Saints [page 108]

The Church is the Communion of Saints. The Church is the unity of all the faithful followers of Jesus on Earth and those in Heaven.

compassion [page 186]

Compassion means to care about others when they are hurt or feeling sad. Having compassion makes us want to help them feel better.

Confirmation [page 146]

Confirmation is the Sacrament in which the gift of the Holy Spirit strengthens us to live our Baptism.

conscience [page 298]

Conscience is a gift from God that helps us to make wise choices.

consequences [page 296]

Consequences are the good or bad things that happen after we make choices.

courage [page 210]

We receive the gift of courage from the Holy Spirit at Baptism. This gift helps us choose to do what is good.

Covenant [page 68]

The Covenant is God's promise to always love and be kind to his people.

covet [page 266]

We covet when we have an unhealthy desire for something.

Creator [page 50]

God alone is the Creator. God made everyone and everything out of love and without any help.

Crucifixion [page 82]

The Crucifixion is the Death of Jesus on a cross.

disciples [page 14]

Disciples are people who follow and learn from someone. Disciples of Jesus follow and learn from him.

Eucharist [page 200]

The Eucharist is the Sacrament of the Body and Blood of Jesus Christ.

F

faith [page 28]

Faith is a gift from God that makes us able to believe in him.

[page 132]

The virtue of faith is a gift from God. It gives us the power to come to know God and believe in him.

false witness [page 268]

Giving false witness means telling lies.

forgiveness [page 156]

Forgiveness is a sign of love. We ask for forgiveness because we love God. We want everything to be right again. We share God's forgiving love with others when we forgive people who hurt us.

fortitude [page 240]

Fortitude is another word for courage. Fortitude helps us stay strong, to do our best, and to do what is right and good when it's hard to do so. The Holy Spirit gives us the gift of fortitude to live the way that God wants us to live.

G

generosity [page 90]

You show generosity when you use the gifts you received from God to help others.

goodness [page 102]

Goodness is a sign that we are living our Baptism. When we are good to people, we show that we know they are children of God. When we are good to people, we honor God.

grace [page 134]

Grace is the gift of God sharing his life with us and helping us live as his children.

Great Commandment [page 244]

The Great Commandment is to love God above all else and to love others as we love ourselves.

H

Heaven [page 288]

Heaven is happiness forever with God and all the Saints.

Holy Trinity [page 38]

The Holy Trinity is one God in Three Divine Persons—God the Father, God the Son, and God the Holy Spirit.

honor [page 48]

When we honor others, we show respect and value them. We honor God because we are proud to be his children.

[page 230]

To honor someone is to treat them with kindness, respect, and love.

hope [page 318]

Hope is trusting that God hears us, cares about us, and will care for us.

hospitality [page 24]

Jesus tells us to treat all people with hospitality. Hospitality helps us welcome others as God's children. It helps us treat others with dignity and respect.

humility [page 282]

Humility helps us to recognize that all we are and all we have come from God. We are humble when we choose to follow God's ways and make them our own.

J

Jesus Christ [page 68]

Jesus Christ is the Son of God. He is the Second Person of the Holy Trinity who became one of us. Jesus is true God and true man.

joy [page 294]

Joy is one of the Fruits of the Holy Spirit. Joy shows that we are thankful for God's love and for all God has made. Joy shows that we enjoy life and delight in making others joyful.

justice [page 264]

We practice justice when we do our very best to always be fair to others.

K

kindness [page 228]

We act with kindness when we do things that show we care. We are kind when we treat other people as we want to be treated.

Kingdom of God [page 320]

The Kingdom of God is also called the Kingdom of Heaven.

knowledge [page 144]

Knowledge is one of the Gifts of the Holy Spirit. Knowledge helps us better hear and understand the meaning of the Word of God.

L

Liturgy of the Eucharist [page 200]

The Liturgy of the Eucharist is the second main part of the Mass. The Church does what Jesus did at the Last Supper.

Liturgy of the Word [page 188]

The Liturgy of the Word is the first main part of the Mass. God speaks to us through readings from the Bible.

love [page 174]

Love is the greatest of all virtues. Love gives us the power to cherish God above all things. It also gives us the power to serve people for the sake of God.

M

Mass [page 176]

The Mass is the most important celebration of the Church. At Mass, we gather to worship God. We listen to God's Word. We celebrate and share in the Eucharist.

mercy [page 66]

Jesus said, "Blessed are people of mercy." Mercy helps us act with kindness toward others, no matter what.

O

obedience [page 252]

Authority is a gift from God. God gives people authority to help us follow God's Laws. People in authority, such as parents and grandparents, teachers and principals, priests and bishops, deserve respect. The virtue of obedience gives us strength to honor and respect people in authority.

P

penance [page 162]

Penance is something we do or say to show we are truly sorry for the choices we made to hurt someone.

Pentecost [page 94]

Pentecost is the day the Holy Spirit came to the disciples of Jesus fifty days after the Resurrection.

piety [page 120]

Piety is a Gift of the Holy Spirit. Piety is the love we have for God. That love makes us want to worship and give God thanks and praise.

procession [page 216]

A procession is people prayerfully walking together. It is a prayer in action.

rabbi [page 242]

Rabbi is a Hebrew word that means teacher.

reconciliation [page 162]

Reconciliation means to become friends again.

respect [page 12]

When we pay attention to what others say to us, we show them respect. Listening is a sign of respect and can help us learn well. Respect for others is a way we show God's love.

Resurrection [page 84]

The Resurrection is God the Father raising Jesus from the dead to new life.

Sacraments [page 124]

The Sacraments are the seven signs of God's love for us that Jesus gave the Church. We share in God's love when we celebrate the Sacraments.

sacrifice [page 78]

You sacrifice when you give up something because you love someone. Jesus sacrificed his life for all people. Followers of Jesus make sacrifices out of love for God and for people.

sanctifying grace [page 135]

Sanctifying grace is the gift of God sharing his life with us.

sin [page 158]

Sin is freely choosing to do or say something we know God does not want us to do or say.

soul [page 38]

Our soul is that part of us that lives forever.

spiritual gifts [page 146]

The Holy Spirit gives us spiritual gifts to help us love and serve other people. We use the spiritual gifts to show our love for God.

T

Ten Commandments [page 254]

The Ten Commandments are the laws that God gave Moses. They teach us to live as God's people. They help us live happy and holy lives.

thankfulness [page 198]

Thankfulness is a big part of who we are as disciples of Jesus. We have received wonderful blessings and gifts. Jesus calls us to be a thankful people.

trust [page 366]

When we trust people, we know we can rely on them. We can depend on them to help us when we are in need.

W

wise choices [page 284]

Wise choices help us to live as followers of God.

wonder [page 36]

Wonder is a Gift of the Holy Spirit. It helps us see God's greatness and discover more about God. It then moves us to praise him.

worship [page 124]

Worship means to honor and love God above all else.

Index

Credits